RESPECTFUL REHABILITATION

CARING FOR YOUR OLD HOUSE

A GUIDE FOR OWNERS AND RESIDENTS

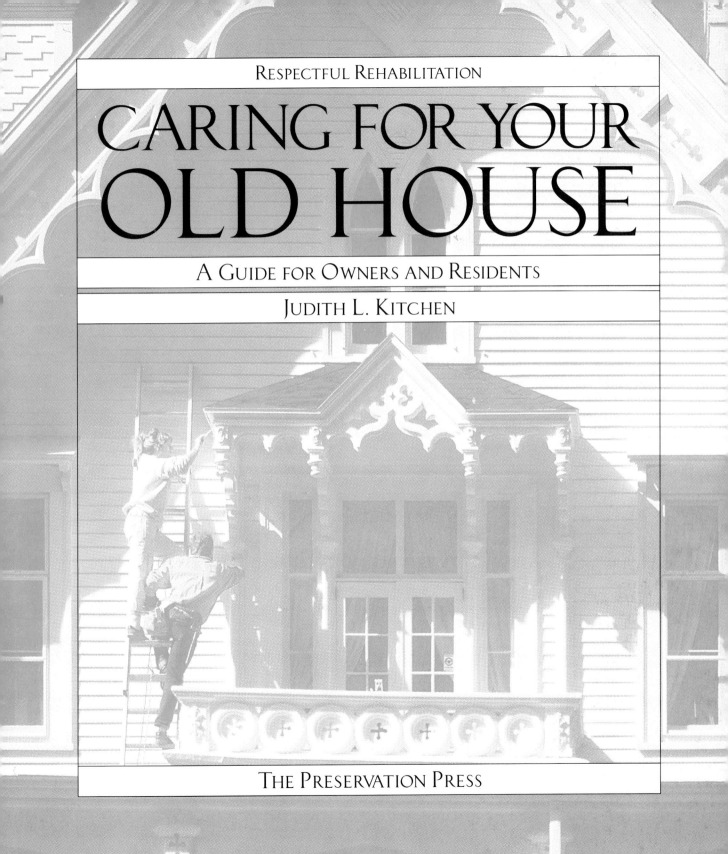

RESPECTFUL REHABILITATION

CARING FOR YOUR OLD HOUSE

A Guide for Owners and Residents

Judith L. Kitchen

THE PRESERVATION PRESS

The Preservation Press
National Trust for Historic Preservation
1785 Massachusetts Avenue, N.W.
Washington, D.C. 20036

The National Trust for Historic Preservation in the United States is the only national, private nonprofit organization chartered by Congress to encourage public participation in the preservation of sites, buildings and objects significant in American history and culture. Support is provided by membership dues, endowment funds, contributions and grants from federal agencies, including the U.S. Department of the Interior, under provisions of the National Historic Preservation Act of 1966. The opinions expressed in this publication do not necessarily reflect the views or policies of the Interior Department. For information about membership, write to the Trust at the above address.

Library of Congress Cataloging-in-Publication Data
Kitchen, Judith L.
    Caring for your old house : a guide for owners and residents /
    Judith L. Kitchen
    p.   cm.   (Respectful rehabilitation)
Includes bibliographical references and index.
ISBN 0-89133-160-3
    1. Dwellings — Maintenance and repair. 2. Historic buildings —
Maintenance and repair.   I. Title. II. Series
TH4817.K58 1990
643'.7—dc20   90-43027

Printed in the United States of America
95 94 93 92   5 4 3 2

∞ The paper used in this publication meets the minimum requirements of the American National Standard for Permanence of Paper for Printed Library Materials Z39.48—1984

Designed and composed in Galliard and Trajan, by Meadows & Wiser, Washington, D.C.

Drawings on page 53 by Richard G. O'Brien of Frank Elmer Associates for *How to Complete the Ohio Historic Inventory,* 1991, by Stephen C. Gordon. Drawings on pages 150, 151, 155 and 185 by Robert D. Loversidge, Jr., AIA, for *Old-Building Owner's Manual,* 1983, by Judith L. Kitchen. Both titles are publications of the Ohio Historic Preservation Office of the Ohio Historical Society.
Cover: The Moses Bulkley House, 1861, a Gothic Revival residence in Southport, Conn. Two conservators finish installing molding on the house's balcony. Generally, two people should not work from one ladder. (© Philip Trager 1989)

CONTENTS

Modest Gothic Revival cottage, Mobile, Ala. The decorated ornament in the gable is an attic vent. (Walter Smalling)

PREFACE

I love old houses. Their attraction and value cannot be disputed. From the grace of a Federal town house and the visual variety of a Queen Anne mansion to the simplicity of a rural I-house and the friendly scale and feel of a Craftsman-style suburban house, old houses have variety and visual appeal, practicality and an unsurpassed sense of time and place. Almost any way I look at it, old houses come out ahead of new ones, no matter how fine the new design or how commodious the space.

I have worked in the field of historic preservation for more than 20 years and during that time have had contact with many property owners, tenants, public officials, organizations and commissions. Over the past two decades attitudes about the benefits of preserving old and historic houses have changed dramatically. The increased cost of raw materials and labor, the visual appeal of historic neighborhoods and their access to city services often lacking in new subdivisions, and the heightened concern for the importance of historic materials and features, all have helped to shape a new and positive awareness of historic resources.

The benefits of preserving historic houses are far reaching, touching the lives of all Americans. Even if we cannot think of any other reason to save them, most old houses are worth preserving solely because of the energy they embody — the energy used in their construction and the energy still present in their foundations, walls, roofs, interior partitions, mechanical systems and ornamentation. Primarily for this reason, it is almost always less expensive to rehabilitate an old house than to build a new one of the same size. Old houses have proven to maintain and increase in value, too.

This book is meant to serve as a general primer on historic preservation for the old-house owner and resident —

Above: Corner of a log house. Insect destruction is evident from the various small holes. (Jack Boucher)

Opposite: Queen Anne house, Denver, with a Palladian window in the gable. (Baird Smith)

to fill the gap between architectural history books and highly technical instruction manuals. It is a book about the many forms of caring for an old house, from researching and possibly nominating it to the National Register of Historic Places, to simply appreciating its fine qualities and its quirks, both obvious and subtle, to specific advice for diagnosing and solving physical problems. The goal is to provide homeowners with a variety of practical methods of preserving the form and details of a historic house and its setting in order to retain the house's essential historic character and appearance, as well as its usefulness.

Although much of the practical information here applies to caring for any old building, the book is primarily about single- and two-family houses and row houses. It also includes houses that have been adapted for other purposes. The book does not cover mobile dwellings, apartment buildings or buildings that were not constructed as houses, even though they may serve as houses today.

The basic approach recommended throughout is a minimalist one — "If it isn't broken, don't fix it." More old houses are destroyed by well-meaning but misguided efforts that lack careful planning and, in the end, waste both money and the house itself. The National Park Service recommends a three-pronged approach to rehabilitation together with consideration of the Secretary of the Interior's Standards for Rehabilitation (see page 31): (1) If the work required goes beyond simple maintenance, the best approach is to repair, not replace, distinctive architectural features and materials. (2) If repair is not possible, because of very severe deterioration, then the form and details of the deteriorated feature or material should dictate the appearance of its replacement. (3) If the original appearance is not known, the replacement feature should be a new design that is visually compatible with the remaining historic features of the house.

This approach to rehabilitation automatically provides a sensitive and sensible course of action. *Caring for Your Old House* will help you fill in the gaps. Most important, it will give you, the homeowner or renter, the background information necessary for you to make reasonable decisions about the approach best for you in caring for your old house and safeguarding a small part of America's heritage.

Judith L. Kitchen

ACKNOWLEDGMENTS

I am most grateful to the National Trust for Historic Preservation and, in particular, Penny Jones, director of preservation programs, and Janet Walker, managing editor, for their ideas and helpful suggestions. They, along with Diane Maddex, former director of The Preservation Press, worked with me to determine the focus and content of this publication, and without them it would not exist.

Thanks also to the Ohio Historical Society for allowing me the time to research and write this book. Franco Ruffini, Ray Luce and Gary Ness were very understanding throughout. My staff cheerfully did extra work. I would like to extend special thanks to the Ohio Historic Preservation Office, and particularly Tom Wolf, for giving me access to project files and photographs and for permitting use of material from two of its publications, the *Old-Building Owner's Manual* (1983) and *Characteristics of Effective Local Historic Preservation Legislation* (1989). In addition, several drawings appear here for the first time but are from the Ohio Historic Inventory manual, soon to be published by the Ohio Historic Preservation Office.

Organizations with which I am involved, such as The Thurber House and the German Village Society, have given me considerable information and knowledge over the years, quite a bit of which appears in this book. Thanks too to those who allowed me to use their old-house photographs.

I thank the citizens of Ohio, in particular, for the opportunity during the last 20-plus years to see firsthand the problems of caring for old houses and the many creative, sensitive solutions that are available and possible. And last, my friends and family have been a mainstay for the duration of this project. For their support and patience I extend special gratitude.

Victorian parlor. (Library of Congress)

Why, What and How to Preserve

Historic preservation in the United States means to preserve the structures, buildings and sites of the past that are significant in American history, architecture and archeology. The preservation of the actual historic materials — the tangible features and parts of the structure or site — is of primary importance in the preservation effort. A replacement or re-creation of part of that material is of little importance, even if it exactly duplicates a historic feature. Consider also the term "historical appearance." It does not have the same meaning as the term "historic." If it did, Main Street at Disneyland, Anaheim, Calif., would be a historic preservation effort. It is, rather, a stage set or backdrop for the activities that occur there. (In the distant future, no doubt, Disneyland will be determined historic in its own right, as it should be.)

Buildings are preserved for many reasons, some of them quite practical, some not. For an increasing number of people, preservation is strictly an economic decision: some financial benefits are available for preserving an old building that are not available for new construction. For others the decision is more an emotional one: a family guarantees the preservation of an ancestral home by placing restrictions on the deed to the property or through the donation of a preservation easement to an organization. For still others, the decision is a practical one: after studying the options, which include a recently constructed suburban home and a lot on which a new home could be built, a young couple decide that an old house in a neighborhood close to work and schools is their best choice. Similarly, for decision makers at all levels of government, historic preservation has proven an essential part of the planning process, offering viable and cost-saving development alternatives.

Above: Row houses in Albany, N.Y., purchased by a local group to prevent their demolition. (Louise McA. Merritt)

Opposite: Swiss Avenue, Dallas, a street of well-maintained old houses. (Carleton Knight III)

Lincoln Home, Springfield, Ill., where archeological work has revealed a number of site and building features, including wells, a cistern, a drainage channel and a furnace system, in addition to a number of Lincoln-era artifacts. (National Park Service)

Key issues in historic preservation have changed during the last 40 years, and they are continuing to change, with more focus today on interiors, the sensitive treatment of original materials, the various periods reflected in buildings, concerns for the environment, the overall quality of life and the true cost of energy and its limited supply. Historic buildings, particularly houses, are seen less as potential museums and more as valuable neighborhood assets, while most historical societies and historic preservation organizations are interested less in owning and administering additional house museums and more in providing advice and assistance to those who can adapt these structures to modern uses.

To begin, let's examine the terms restoration, reconstruction and rehabilitation. Current trends in historic preservation are directed toward rehabilitation and away from reconstruction and even from restoration; both can be costly in terms of research and construction and may result in the destruction of a structure's historic fabric in order to return to an earlier period. In the end, the restoration may result in a structure that is historical in appearance only.

For decades a major debate in the field has been waged over the question, How much tampering with historic building materials and features is too much? This controversy began in 19th-century Europe, where such anti-restorationists as John Ruskin, William Morris and Victor Hugo battled with some of the most influential architects and owners, including national governments, over the extent of work to historic buildings, arguing against the destruction of later additions and alterations to historic cathedrals, monasteries and other buildings. These men and their followers believed that each generation is caretaker of the past and has no right to tamper with significant historic buildings. They believed, as many preservationists do today, that buildings, like living things, grow and develop and that to restore them to their original appearance is to destroy them.

To restore a house to an exact period requires a great deal of information about the actual historical appearance of the building; educated guesses, from the design of a living room's crown molding to the massing of an early kitchen wing, produce only building decoration rather than restoration. At one time, this conjectural approach, at least

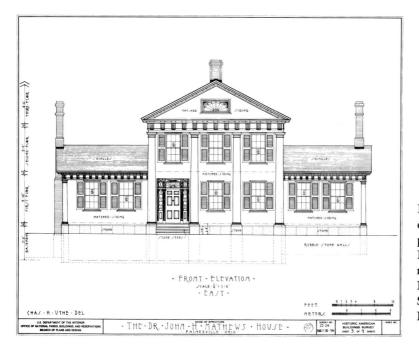

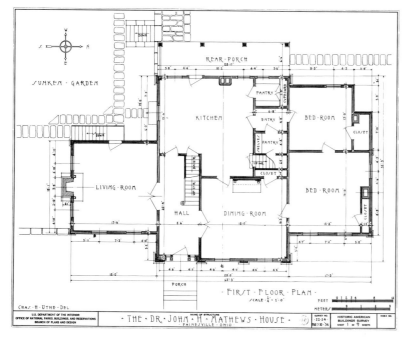

Elevation of the facade and drawing of the first floor plan, Dr. John H. Mathews House, Painesville, Ohio, made in 1934 through the Historic American Buildings Survey. (Charles H. Uthe, HABS)

for some missing features of a historic house, was more acceptable than it is today. As new methods of preserving building materials are developed, as the professions of architectural history, historic archeology and historic preservation

Top: Common energy-saving feature. Doors with operable transoms allow for light and ventilation and permit closing off areas of the house during periods of extreme heat or cold.

Above: Modest old houses preserved primarily because they are still useful.

A Dozen Sensible Reasons to Preserve an Old House

1. Avoid waste. Very simply, why waste something that is still basically sound and usable? With surprisingly few exceptions, old buildings, especially houses, are in good condition structurally. It's a fact — they don't build them like they used to! Would you throw away a good shirt with a missing button? Most people would not.

2. Conserve energy. National studies have shown that on average it takes less energy to rehabilitate an old building than to build a new one. Moreover, old buildings, because of better thermal efficiency, generally require less energy to heat, cool and ventilate than do new buildings. A majority of old houses have inherent energy-saving features, such as porches and wide overhangs, shutters, rooms that can be shut off during periods of extreme heat or cold and transoms for ventilation between rooms.

3. Save money. Historic preservation has numerous financial benefits over new construction. It generally costs less to repair than to replace or build new. Also, an owner can often live in an old house while rehabilitation work is under way, thereby saving the cost of temporary housing.

4. Make money. With the federal tax credit currently available for certified rehabilitation work to an income-producing certified historic structure, including rental housing, the cost of rehabilitation can be far less than the cost for a similarly sized new house.

5. Learn from the past. The past is our best source of information about what works, what does not, what looks good, what does not, and, most important, how we developed as a nation and as a culture.

6. Retain a sense of continuity with the past. Cultural development is a continuum. Without all the parts — including old houses — it is impossible to piece together an accurate picture of what and who we Americans are.

7. Maintain variety in our environment. Visual variety adds immeasurably to the richness and enjoyment of our surroundings.

8. Educate future generations. Would you want your chidren and grandchildren to be able to see and experience historic houses only in books and other printed materials? Something that is three-dimensional, such as the architecture and the artifacts of a culture, must be experienced firsthand to be experienced at all.

9. Enrich the overall quality of life. Quality of life is determined by many factors, including physical environment. Old houses and established neighborhoods often have advantages not found elsewhere. Among these are easily accessible mass transportation, proximity to city services, workplaces and shopping; a rich mix of ages, ethnic groups and economic levels; an established parks and recreation system; and, not least, mature trees.

10. Alleviate local unemployment problems. Because historic preservation work tends to be very labor intensive, more of the construction dollars spent for rehabilitation work than those spent for new construction go directly to creating and maintaining jobs at the city or village level, thereby helping to lower local unemployment.

11. Prevent the extinction of certain styles of buildings and types of building crafts. Unless the actual historic examples are available for use as an educational tool and guide, teaching and learning a craft such as early forms of metalworking or wood joinery may be impossible.

12. Preserve the setting of another building or site. A building's setting is a crucial part of its character. All too often, a historic house loses its neighbors and becomes, in a sense, orphaned. It helps to think of historic buildings in neighborhoods, not just as a series of individual significant structures.

Facade of the Federal-style James Watson House (right) in Lower Manhattan's Financial District, the sole survivor of the fine early mansions in that part of New York City.

15

mature, and as techniques of nondestructive testing are discovered, perhaps buildings such as Independence Hall in Philadelphia will no longer be subjected to several attempts at "authentic" restoration. Those of us who are able to consider purchasing or renting an old or historic home follow a strategy of rehabilitation — preserving the existing historic features and materials, while making only necessary changes to support modern conveniences and uses.

HISTORIC PRESERVATION IN THE UNITED STATES

Since the beginning of the historic preservation movement in this country, preservation has occurred for at least one of five distinct motivations. These impelling reasons, each important for preserving buildings today, are, in the order they appeared: association with a historical event or person; architectural significance; public involvement; economic benefits; and local planning.

HISTORICAL ASSOCIATIONS

Nearly everyone knows of a significant house or an event connected with a property or has heard about a group responsible for the well-being of a special structure. Examples of historically significant properties, such as Mount Vernon (1754–99) and the Gettysburg Battlefield (1863), exist in every state. While landmark houses such as Monticello (1769–1809) and The Hermitage (1835), for example, are of considerable architectural significance, campaigns for their preservation were waged not for their architecture but because of their association with famous Americans — Thomas Jefferson and Andrew Jackson.

Beginning in the late 19th century, diligent efforts by volunteer organizations such as the Daughters of the American Revolution and the National Society of Colonial Dames of America resulted in the preservation of numerous houses and also other buildings associated with individuals who played a part in the early history of the nation. These groups struggled with the question of how to use a building once it has been acquired or otherwise saved. Properties were expected to be museums, eventually administered by

Mount Vernon in 1855 (above) and today (left).

the federal, state or local government. In reality, government played a minor role. Most buildings acquired for preservation still were established as museums, but they were administered by the local volunteer organization through a curatorial "staff" of interested volunteers. Historic homes became "house museums" and were furnished, accordingly, with as many items as possible from the notable person commemorated by the structure. Sponsoring organizations quickly discovered that most of these house museums were major money drains. In fact, only two or three house museums have ever made a profit.

Other buildings attracted attention because of their architectural significance: they were the only, earliest or best example of a particular style or type. These examples were artistically important; they either exemplified fine craftsmanship or design or were aesthetically pleasing or innovative. Rather than the volunteers who came to the rescue of homes of famous persons, those who directed this type of preservation effort tended to be historians and historical societies, museums and architects. One important example is the Octagon, built in 1801 in Washington, D.C., and acquired in 1901 by the American Institute of Architects. Although the house certainly played an important historical role, the motivation for its preservation was primarily its architectural significance.

Buildings preserved for their architecture also were made into museums, but the fit with the organization was often better, since many of the owner-preservers already were historical societies, preservation organizations, such as the Society for the Preservation of New England Antiquities, or were established as museums themselves.

The Octagon (1801), Washington, D.C., as it appeared in the 1880s (left) and after construction of the headquarters building of the American Institute of Architects behind it (right). (American Institute of Architects Foundation)

PUBLIC INVOLVEMENT

In l926 John D. Rockefeller, Jr., decided to finance the restoration of Virginia's decaying colonial capital, the city of Williamsburg, marking a turning point in the annals of historic preservation. Williamsburg, as a museum village, set an example: it gave visitors an idea of the aesthetic benefits of living in cohesive historic neighborhoods. Since then, historic preservation efforts have changed dramatically and permanently, extending well beyond single buildings to embrace entire historic residential neighborhoods and commercial districts such as Georgetown in Washington, D.C., and Pioneer Square in Seattle.

In the 1950s and 1960s, the movement still was not strong enough or large enough to prevent the excesses of federally assisted urban renewal programs. Buildings were demolished at an alarming rate, leaving entire inner-city areas devastated; few inner-city communities escaped demo-

Street in Colonial Williamsburg, the museum village that made many visitors realize the value of historical resources, especially as these resources worked together.

Above left: Historic photograph of Saxton House (c.1841, c.1865), Canton, Ohio, girlhood home of Ida Saxton McKinley, wife of President William McKinley. The McKinleys lived in this house from 1873 to 1892. (Ohio Historic Preservation Office)

Above right: Saxton House as it appeared in 1978, before restoration. The Second Empire–style house had served a variety of uses over the years and was barely recognizable under the insensitive additions. In this case, restoration was an appropriate approach. (Ohio Historic Preservation Office)

Right: Saxton House today. The project, slated for commercial use following completion, qualified for a federal rehabilitation tax credit. (Tim Richardson)

lition. The National Trust for Historic Preservation, chartered in 1949 by the U.S. Congress to be, for the first time, a united, national voice for historic preservation, could speak out on the issues and helped gradually to increase public involvement, but nothing could halt the destruction completely. Slowly, urban planners recognized that wholesale replacement of historic housing and commercial structures with new buildings did not necessarily solve problems. Often, old problems still existed and new ones were created. This wholesale demolition of our cities did help Americans realize that old neighborhoods had amenities and visual appeal lacking in areas of new housing.

Crucial to increased public awareness of the benefits of preserving old buildings was the passage of the National

Historic Preservation Act of 1966. This law created today's comprehensive national historic preservation program, housed in the National Park Service of the U.S. Department of the Interior, with the states as the federal government's partners in safeguarding historic resources. Under the law and its amendments, any federally assisted project must first be reviewed to determine its effect on properties listed in or eligible for listing in the National Register of Historic Places, a roster of significant properties across the United States. The 1966 law broadened the federal government's concept of what could be considered historic to include properties of state or local, as well as national, significance. This change is primarily responsible for the popularity and success of the National Register program and for much of the grass-roots success of historic preservation work in this country.

Beginning in the late 1960s, the historic preservation effort aligned itself with the back-to-the-city movement, and its popularity soared. Isolated examples of neighborhood preservation such as Georgetown gave way to almost an epidemic of preservation activity as city after city saw "urban pioneers" taking boards off old buildings and returning neighborhoods to their forgotten vibrancy. Anybody now could live in a historic house and appreciate it as a vital part of the community. By the early 1970s, this movement had produced negative overtones as well; property became more valuable; taxes went up; and renters left, often against their own will.

Two other events also helped to shape public awareness, the energy crisis of the mid-1970s, which highlighted the inherent energy-saving features of old buildings, and the U.S. Bicentennial of 1976. From civic organizations to youth groups, many people quickly found that a hands-on approach to preserving a local landmark was fun and more rewarding than reading history books.

ECONOMIC BENEFITS

The emphasis on the economic benefits of historic preservation activity in the United States can be dated to the passage of the Tax Reform Act of 1976. For the first time in the history of United States tax policy, an economic

The Battery, part of the Old and Historic District in Charleston, S.C., showing the area's distinctive stacked-porch style.

incentive was offered to investors who chose to rehabilitate income-producing historic structures that met certain standards ensuring that the character and significant elements of the buildings were preserved (see the Secretary of the Interior's Standards for Rehabilitation, pages 31–33). Generally, any buildings listed in the National Register of Historic Places could qualify. Until 1986 this law and the several that followed have strengthened historic preservation incentives and resulted in the rehabilitation of thousands of historic structures in the United States, the vast majority of which, according to their owners, would not have received a second look without the investment tax credit for rehabilitation.

By focusing on an economic advantage to preservation, the movement for the first time attracted widespread attention from individuals and organizations with the money to rehabilitate historic buildings, particularly the larger commercial structures in urban areas. At the same time a dilemma arose for some preservationists: those making the investment often cared more about the economics of a project than its historic fabric. Nevertheless, most preservationists would agree that the tax credits and other incentives have saved more than they have hurt. Progress, however, has been slowed by the Tax Reform Act of 1986, which, while not eliminating the rehabilitation tax credit, made investments in historic property far less appealing to investors by removing or lessening many of the financial incentives.

LOCAL PLANNING

Led by Charleston, S.C., in 1931, some older, larger cities had, by the early 1970s, enacted special ordinances to ensure that any changes to the appearance of the buildings in designated historic areas adhered to specific guidelines designed to protect the significant historical and architectural qualities of the districts.

Today, all major cities and many hundreds of smaller communities are including historic preservation concerns as a normal, routine part of their planning efforts. As a result, many old and historic buildings, including houses, are being identified, studied, rehabilitated and reused. Also, cooperative efforts between local governments, private individuals and historic preservation organizations are developing creative ways to achieve mutual goals through historic preservation, and local financial incentives are gaining in popularity. One tangible result is the success of the National Main Street Center program operated by the National Trust for Historic Preservation.

In 1980 the National Historic Preservation Act was amended to increase the potential role of local governments in the historic preservation partnership. Under the law, certified local governments (CLGs) must include historic preservation as a significant element of their local planning efforts, working toward the development of specific historic preservation plans for their communities and protecting archeologically, historically and architecturally significant districts and individual properties. Although it has been slow in developing, the CLG program is becoming a significant element in regional and statewide historic preservation planning, serving as a major historic preservation incentive in many communities.

Timeline

1816
Old State House (Independence Hall) purchased by the city of Philadelphia.

1850
Hasbrouck House, Newburgh, N.Y., General George Washington's headquarters, purchased by the state of New York as the first house museum in the United States.

1856
The Hermitage, Nashville, home of Andrew Jackson, purchased by the state of Tennessee.

1858
Mount Vernon, Mount Vernon, Va., home of George Washington, purchased by the Mount Vernon Ladies' Association of the Union, led by Ann Pamela Cunningham.

1863
Governor John Hancock House, Boston, demolished following extensive efforts to preserve it. Before its demolition, however, measured drawings of the building were made.

1888
Association for the Preservation of Virginia Antiquities founded in Richmond.

1891
Trustees of Public Reservations (Mass.) incorporated and becomes a model for the British (1894) and American (1949) national trusts.

1895
American Scenic and Historic Preservation Society formed primarily to administer historic properties, most of them houses, in New York State. This organization existed well into the 20th century.

1901
The Octagon, Washington, D.C., the 1801 Federal-style home of John and Ann Tayloe, designed by William Thornton, acquired by the American Institute of Architects.

1906
Antiquities Act, first major federal preservation legislation, passed to impose restrictions on the removal or destruction of archeological sites on federal property and provide for presidential designation of national monuments on federal land.

1910
Society for the Preservation of New England Antiquities founded in Boston by William Sumner Appleton.

In general, if you feel that an old house has historical importance or if you like the way it looks, then it is probably worth considering for preservation. Getting involved in historic preservation is as simple as that! While choosing a suitable building can pose some difficulties (see Before You Begin), it is very important to realize from the outset that not every old house can be successfully or sensitively adapted to every lifestyle or to every use.

Other criteria more specific than simply liking a home because it is old will be helpful, particularly if you must convince someone else that the building should be preserved. If the house meets or appears to meet the criteria for listing in the National Register of Historic Places (see page 73), then it is definitely worthy of consideration for preservation. The same is true of buildings that meet the criteria for listing in a state register or a local landmarks register, either individually or as part of a historic district.

A list of houses that have been preserved throughout the United States would include such diverse examples as company houses in Pullman, Ill., and Youngstown, Ohio, antebellum plantations in the South, adobe dwellings in the Southwest, sod houses in the Dakotas, the distinctive row houses of Hoboken, N.J., Baltimore and Philadelphia, and Native American dwellings in the Northwest and Alaska.

The types of buildings chosen for preservation have changed dramatically over the years. Not surprisingly, the first houses to receive attention were the oldest — those built during the colonial or territorial years. More recently, Victorian period buildings, those constructed in the latter half of the 19th century, have been recognized as significant, both historically and visually. Now, houses built in the early years of the 20th century are being recognized as significant and irreplaceable. This recent trend encompasses bungalows and Craftsman houses, among others. Once only the largest, most lavish, high-style houses were preserved, but historic dwellings representing every segment of society — including mail-order houses, such as those sold by Sears, Roebuck and Company — are being recognized as significant today. All styles, all ages, all prices and all locations, as well as all features of a building — the exterior and the gardens, landscaping and site, as well as the interior — are being preserved. At one time, historic preservation efforts focused primarily on the exteriors of historic houses, but now interiors are receiving equal attention.

DEMYSTIFYING TERMINOLOGY

Approaches to preservation are varied and wide-ranging, as demonstrated by the following annotated list of the approaches taken over the years — some highly recommended and others strongly advised against. Rarely will a project encompass only one of these approaches; a combination of two or more approaches is more likely. Careful planning and a clear understanding of the procedures involved to achieve the desired preservation result are necessary.

The terms "preservation" and "historic preservation" are used generically to mean any work designed to assist in the conservation of the historic fabric and features of an old building. Such work could range from basic research to the actual repair of the building and its parts.

The first six approaches are important tools to use to achieve preservation, but they do not actually result in the physical conservation of the house. Approaches seven through nine, if not followed by one of the later treatments, will eventually result in the deterioration of the house because they do not involve maintenance work. Generally speaking, approaches 10 through 12 are recommended, for they involve little or no tampering with or destruction of historic building materials or parts.

Judging from recent trends, it appears that the vast majority, possibly 90 percent or more, of all work to a historic house falls under rehabilitation, approach 11. Restoration, approach 13, carries some danger, in that later, significant architectural fabric may need to be destroyed in order to return the house to its appearance at a specific earlier date. This approach is rarely recommended by today's preservation professionals and especially the National Park Service. Approaches 14 through 17 — remodeling, reconstruction, relocation and salvage — carry real dangers, noted in their descriptions, and are included here only to illustrate the range of changes to which some

1916
National Park Service founded by act of Congress, becoming caretaker of nine national monuments.

1923
Monticello, near Charlottesville, Va., home of Thomas Jefferson, acquired by the Thomas Jefferson Memorial Foundation.

1926
Williamsburg, Va., colonial capital of that state, targeted for preservation through the financial support of John D. Rockefeller, Jr., and the efforts of William A. R. Goodwin, rector of Bruton Parish Church, Williamsburg.

1931
First local historic district ordinance in the United States passed in Charleston, S.C., establishing the Old and Historic District.

1933
Battlefields and other historic federal property transferred to the National Park Service.

Historic American Buildings Survey begun as a New Deal program to employ out-of-work architects in preparing measured drawings of historic buildings, including numerous houses. This innovative program has served as a model for other countries.

houses have been subjected and which should be avoided.

1. Identification, by means of a survey, is a vital first step, for it provides basic data, such as the building's location, style, type and date. Without this initial research and inventory effort, no historic preservation planning could take place.

2. Listing consists of nominating and registering the property in a local landmarks list, a state historic properties list or the National Register of Historic Places. This provides, at each level, a different measure of protection. (See pages 66–70 for a description of each type of listing.)

3. Zoning is a means by which houses and other properties are protected at the local level. In this country the strongest historic preservation laws exist at the local level. Individual houses and historic districts of houses are designated as significant and worthy of preservation. Property owners must follow specific guidelines and be issued a certificate of appropriateness before any work may be undertaken. Many variations in historic zoning ordinances are possible, and a number of types of local ordinances have proven to be successful. (See pages 70–83 for further discussion on local design review.)

4. Acquisition includes not only simply buying a house but also acquiring easements and transferring development rights. Believed by some to be the surest of all the preservation approaches, outright purchase is one of the least practical, as few can afford all the buildings, structures and sites we would like to see preserved. Partial ownership — in the form of easements and other deed restrictions — is an important alternative to full ownership. (See pages 71–75 for more information on easements and the transfer of development rights.)

5. Documentation consists of preparing measured drawings, photographs and a narrative explanation of the construction history of the house. While documentation is valuable for archival research and reconstruction purposes, it does not preserve the house itself. A good example is the saga of the John Hancock House in Boston. Before the house was demolished in 1863, measured drawings were carefully prepared in anticipation of a later reconstruction. Planned and discussed for many years, the reconstruction never took place. Now, however, the drawings are quite valuable to architectural historians for study purposes. Documentation is also of special value when properties have suffered damage from fire, tornado, flood or other disasters.

6. Marking the property can mean simply placing a plaque or marker on the house or elsewhere on the property designating it a historic structure and giving the date, builder's name and, sometimes, other relevant information. A property owner may choose this approach to announce that the house is listed in the National Register of Historic Places; often neighborhood or historic district organizations will offer markers to their members to place on historic homes or erect them at major entrances to historic districts. Such efforts as a walking tour or a published guide to the houses are effective in complementing the marking program.

7. Benign neglect means to most preservationists that the house is not being torn down and perhaps that some minimal work is being done to keep it standing a little while longer.

1980
Amendments to the National Historic Preservation Act passed fostering a strengthened local role in preservation activities.

1981
Economic Recovery Tax Act of 1981 gives investors significant new incentives in preserving historic structures — a 25 percent tax credit for certified rehabilitation work to income-producing certified historic buildings.

1985
San Francisco adopts a downtown master plan with the strongest design controls yet devised in an American city, including the protection of more than 250 landmark buildings.

1986
Tax Reform Act of 1986 passed reducing the historic preservation tax credit to 20 percent and imposing new passive income and loss rules to real estate activity.

Row of historic houses against the city skyline in San Francisco, where historic preservation is a vital part of city and neighborhood planning. (Carleton Knight III)

Neglected, isolated historic house, still a relatively common scene in many areas. (Ohio Historic Preservation Office)

8. Protection includes such measures as boarding up windows, installing fire protection and security systems or simply covering a hole in the roof temporarily with plastic.

9. Stabilization includes measures designed to ensure the structural stability of a house that is damaged or deteriorated. Stabilization work includes rebuilding a damaged section of a foundation or carefully drawing a bowed wall back into place.

10. Maintenance, which is sometimes called, simply, basic preservation, consists of the continuing care and repair of a house.

11. Rehabilitation includes work to make a property usable and useful for a contemporary function while taking necessary measures to preserve features that are historically and visually significant. "Renovation" sometimes is used incorrectly to describe rehabilitation projects.

12. Adaptive use is a type of rehabilitation in which the resulting use is wholly or partly different from the building's original function. Any new use that destroys the architectural character of the old house is to be avoided. Unfortunately, for example, numerous early 19th-century houses that originally had a number of small rooms have been opened up by new owners to create larger reception areas and offices or even larger family living spaces. On the

Two once-identical houses. The house on the left has been remodeled to such an extent it is barely discernible as a historic house. (David Taylor)

other hand, some old houses seem to serve better in their new, sensitively adapted uses than they ever did as dwellings! The best adaptive use, however, is the one that requires the fewest changes to the house and destroys none of the historic fabric. "Retrofitting" sometimes is used to describe adaptive-use projects.

13. Restoration means to return a house to its appearance at a particular period of time, often when it was first built, removing everything that was not there originally. Strictly speaking, restoration is an all or nothing approach. In other words, if a house is to be restored to its 1830 state, then the electricity, indoor plumbing, central heating and other modern features must be removed and replaced with whatever was there in 1830. This approach is not considered appropriate to preservation and is often highly discouraged. It destroys much of a house's significant later history, and, even if the house is restored to a given period, much of what appears historic is only a re-creation of what was there originally.

14. Remodeling consists of greater and, therefore, even more inappropriate change than that permitted in rehabilitation projects. It means that architecturally and historically significant features are altered, resulting in destruction rather than preservation. Remodeling has meant gutting a building's interior, for example, while preserving the exterior, leaving nothing more than a facade or historic container. Exteriors can be remodeled too, perhaps with inappropriate covering materials.

15. Reconstruction calls for rebuilding a vanished house or a major section of a house, using accurate documentation of its appearance. Note that this approach calls for careful documentation of the original house; conjecture will not do. The reconstructed house or section of the house is historic only in appearance.

16. Relocation, or moving, is the process of transferring a building to another foundation nearby or distant from its original site. Buildings have been moved since the nation was founded. Moving can be accomplished by lifting the house and transporting it by flatbed truck to another site intact or by dismantling it and moving it piece by piece. However, every building has a close relationship with its original site and setting, and moving, by definition, alters this relationship. Also, a transplanted building must have a new foundation, perhaps of reused masonry from the old

Moving a house, the last option in saving a building.

site but still newly constructed, or reconstructed, so part of the historic fabric will be lost. Moving buildings, including historic houses, is today regarded as a last-resort preservation process, undertaken when all efforts at preserving the building *in situ* have failed.

17. Salvage is often used as a last-resort to save significant parts or pieces of the house or archeological artifacts from its site by carefully removing them, perhaps before the demolition of the building itself, to display them in a museum or reuse them in another building. This process is controversial, and few preservationists regard it as a viable historic preservation measure. Regrettably, the demand for such decorative old-house items as stained-glass windows, ornate doors, mantels and stairways has, in fact, caused the sale, removal and even theft of such items from houses in some neighborhoods. Sometimes these items reappear as decorative artifacts in theme restaurants or are reinstalled inappropriately in other old houses or even in new ones. The reuse of historic building parts and materials in this manner is not preservation.

REHABILITATION STANDARDS AND GUIDELINES

The secretary of the interior, as head of the chief federal preservation agency, has codified a set of 10 rehabilitation standards with accompanying guidelines for federal projects. The standards and guidelines are used by preservationists across the country and have been widely adopted by states and communities as sound principles in preserving old buildings.

Initially established to evaluate work on properties listed in the National Register of Historic Places, the standards, updated in 1990 but unchanged in meaning, also are used as a basis for certifying eligibility for the federal rehabilitation tax credit for income-producing historic properties.

The guidelines that accompany the standards are advisory in intent and provide examples of rehabilitation activities that are recommended or not recommended. For instance, they recommend "inspecting painted wood surfaces to determine whether repainting is necessary or if cleaning is all that is required" but don't recommend "removing paint that is firmly adhering to and thus protecting wood surfaces."

THE SECRETARY OF THE INTERIOR'S

STANDARDS FOR REHABILITATION

1. A property shall be used for its historic purpose or be placed in a new use that requires minimal change to the defining characteristics of the building and its site and environment.

2. The historic character of a property shall be retained and preserved. The removal of historic materials or alteration of features and spaces that characterize a property shall be avoided.

3. Each property shall be recognized as a physical record of its time, place and use. Changes that create a false sense of historical development, such as adding conjectural features or architectural elements from other buildings, shall not be undertaken.

4. Most properties change over time; those changes that have acquired historic significance in their own right shall be retained and preserved.

5. Distinctive features, finishes and construction techniques or examples of craftsmanship that characterize a historic property shall be preserved.

6. Deteriorated historic features shall be repaired rather than replaced. Where the severity of deterioration requires replacement of a distinctive feature, the new feature shall match the old in design, color, texture and other visual qualities and, where possible, materials. Replacement of missing features shall be substantiated by documentary, physical or pictorial evidence.

7. Chemical or physical treatments, such as sandblasting, that cause damage to historic materials shall not be used. The surface cleaning of structures, if appropriate, shall be undertaken using the gentlest means possible.

8. Significant archeological resources affected by a project shall be protected and preserved. If such resources must be disturbed, mitigation measures shall be undertaken.

9. New additions, exterior alterations or related new construction shall not destroy historic materials that characterize the property. The new work shall be differentiated from the old and shall be compatible with the massing, size, scale and architectural features to protect the historic integrity of the property and its environment.

10. New additions and adjacent or related new construction shall be undertaken in such a manner that if removed in the future, the essential form and integrity of the historic property and its environment would be unimpaired.

THE FUTURE OF PRESERVATION

Saving buildings, whether homes or factories, offices or apartments, has become more than a pastime for many Americans. While the field of historic preservation continues to attract dedicated volunteers, many have gone on to become professionals in this growing discipline. As development encroaches on the areas many hold sacred, more new converts understand the importance of preserving what is here rather than eagerly awaiting what is to come.

Historic preservation attracts more of us concerned both with saving our country's architectural and cultural heritage as well as conserving its resources. And preservation becomes a practical solution as resources become more and more scarce and as periodicals such as *The Old-House Journal* educate and inform about old houses and the proper ways to care for them. As standards for preservation projects, such as the Secretary of the Interior's Standards for Rehabilitation, are used more widely and understood at all levels of preservation activity, sensitively preserved houses become the norm, rather than the exception.

The movement gains strength by developing alliances with business and urban interests and even rural concerns. As more and more towns and cities see the value of preserving their Main Streets and neighborhoods, historic preservation becomes a movement for the many rather than the few. Historic preservation has become and will continue to be an integral part of American life.

LEARNING ABOUT OLD HOUSES

The study of architectural styles has not always been popular. Roughly between 1915 and 1955 many architectural educators believed that rigorous study of historical architectural styles and, in particular, classical architectural forms, would lead to slavish copying of past building forms and details. Others felt that each historical style had already been expressed as excellently and completely as possible and, therefore, any new effort would be second rate. Whatever the motivation, architectural styles were not stressed in architectural history courses and often were ignored altogether. It was during this period, specifically 1925–50, that the International Style with its sleek steel, and column-less, glass-encased structures found so much favor.

Before and following this period, the study of historic architecture has occupied a more significant place in American architectural education. And today, architectural forms of the past are celebrated in many of the best-known new buildings. Direct reference to past style in the form of columns, pilasters, pediments and other classical forms is common and has come to be known as postmodern architecture.

Above: Atlas illustration of the same residence in Marietta from the 1870s. (Titus, Simmons & Titus, Philadelphia)

VALUE OF ARCHITECTURAL STYLE

Architectural style is the outward manifestation of an underlying design philosophy formed by a complex set of social, political and economic factors. Through style we can study and understand the development of building forms and ornamentation and learn valuable clues by which to date buildings. Most of the buildings studied in art and architectural history classes are high-

Opposite: Gothic Revival mansion in Marietta, Ohio, in the 1970s. (Ohio Historic Preservation Office)

Vernacular example of a Second Empire home. The porch most likely is not original.

style buildings, buildings that exhibit the characteristics of a particular identifiable national or regional architectural style.

No more than 20 percent of all the houses in this country are high-style buildings. Why, then, do we devote so much energy and time to the study of this minority? Mainly because, by their very nature, these buildings are and have always been on the cutting edge of design. They are considered by many to be architecture at its highest level. They are indisputably the best of one major element of architectural design — style. More important, they represent the sources of the design forms and motifs used in the vast majority of other buildings. These can be thought of as popular or vernacular versions of the prevailing high styles, and they appear to exist for every one of the major styles of architecture.

These vernacular structures make up the majority of houses in this country, and they fall between high-style and folk architecture, which in its purest form exhibits no element of any style. The design inspiration for folk, or traditional, architecture derives from building traditions of a particular locale, not from outside sources, as with high-style architecture, whose design inspiration can come from existing, older buildings, design expositions and information about ancient buildings that may appear in books and magazines.

Knowledge of the characteristics of a particular style enables one to date houses in that style fairly precisely, at least to the decade. Keep in mind that the dates of the styles differ somewhat throughout the various sections of the country. Obviously houses built in identifiable styles are the easiest to date. An examination of the form and details of such a building can reveal the inspiration for the design; a next step would be to research what information was available to the designer. Designs can be traced by the appearance of a particular magazine article, for example. The popularity of the Egyptian Revival style in the period 1830–50 can be attributed, at least in part, to the publication of an article entitled "Egyptian Architecture," which appeared in the March 1829 issue of *The American Quarterly Review*, published in Philadelphia.

Style alone is a dangerous way to approach the study of historic houses, however, because it gives only a limited amount of data about the building. Also, style does not necessarily indicate anything about the building's structural system. It also does not often indicate what materials were used in constructing the house or anything about its location or setting, all of which are essential elements in the study and understanding of American architecture.

TWENTY-ONE COMMON OLD-HOUSE STYLES

The major American house styles are listed here in the general order of their appearance, with the dates of their greatest popularity and short descriptions.

■ **Spanish Colonial (1620–1855)**
One story, or sometimes two stories, with low roof
Full-length porch or veranda
Adobe or stuccoed stone construction
Projecting timbers
Examples in areas of the southern United States occupied
    by Spain

■ **Georgian (1690–1780)**
Two-story, rigidly symmetrical, rectilinear form
Steeply pitched hipped or gable roof, often with dormers

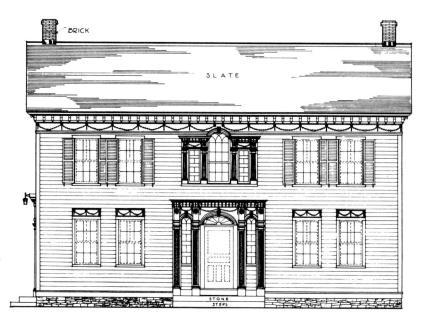

Right: Federal-style house, Castleton, Vt. (W. Tarbell, HABS)

Below: Brice House, c. 1766–73, Annapolis, Md., a Georgian dwelling with a number of dependencies. (M. E. Warren)

Palladian Renaissance details, including formal
  entrances, porticoes and ornate mantelpieces
Often multipart, consisting of a central house with flanking
  smaller dependencies
Examples in 13 original colonies

- **Federal (1780–1830)**

Two- or three-story square or rectangular forms with
  vertical emphasis sometimes with curved or polygonal
  projections
Low-pitched roof
Delicately executed classical Roman details on exterior and
  interior
Gracefully curved fanlight over entrance
Interior spaces sometimes round, oval or polygonal in form
Vernacular examples: possibly having only the characteristic
  porch or entrance fanlight

- **Jeffersonian (1780–1830)**

Square forms commonly of red brick with white-painted
  wood trim
Classical Roman orders, massive and unfussy
Colonnaded, arcaded or porticoed facade
Low roof
Examples in the South, especially Virginia

- **Greek Revival (1800–70)**

Rectangular block forms with horizontal emphasis and no
  projections
Low roof
Classical Greek orders, heavy and simple
Columns and pilasters
Vernacular examples: possibly having no columns, exhibit-
  ing the style through proportion, form and massing

**Greek Revival homes in
Mobile, Ala.**

- **Gothic Revival (1820–90)**

Picturesque asymmetry, with vertical emphasis
Gothic details such as towers, crenellation, steep gable
  roofs, bay and oriel windows
Pointed-arch windows and doorways
Fancy jigsawn ornamentation, such as bargeboards
Later examples: polychromatic with heavier and more exu-
  berant ornamentation

Right: Stick Style house, Newport, R.I. (J. Chimura, HABS)

Below left: Italianate town house in Cleveland. (Ohio Historic Preservation Office)

Below right: Gothic Revival example in Cincinnati. (Miami Purchase Association)

Vernacular examples: basic characteristics, such as board-and-batten siding and detailed wooden trim

■ **Italianate (1840–90)**
Low roof with pronounced cornice supported on brackets
Rounded or flat-topped windows with projecting hoodmolds

Italian Villa examples: towers and often with arcaded
   porches and balustraded balconies
Later examples: polychromatic with more ornamentation
Vernacular examples: usually having only brackets or perhaps modest hoodmolds over the windows

■ Second Empire (1860–90)

Three-dimensional effect achieved by projections and
   small-scaled classical ornamentation
Mansard roof with dormers
Tall, ornate chimneys
Vernacular examples: mansard roofs only

■ Stick Style (1860–90)

Sticklike exterior ornamentation expressing the structure
   underneath
Steep, intersecting gable roofs
Angular, vertical, asymmetrical forms
Porches and verandas

■ Queen Anne (1875–1900)

Asymmetrical massing of form, often with a tower or turret
   and ornate chimneys
Intersecting steep gable roofs
Small-scaled ornamentation
Variety of materials, shapes and colors in the same building
Bay and oriel windows
Ornate porches and garrets
Open floor plan with prominent stairway
Vernacular examples: sometimes called Princess Anne, hav-
   ing irregular massing, a high roof and some characteris-
   tic ornamentation
Eastlake examples: heavy, three-dimensional porch or
   house ornamentation consisting of curved brackets,
   spindles and turned posts

■ Richardsonian Romanesque (1875–1900)

Heavy stone construction with horizontal emphasis and
   variations in texture and color
Gable roof with wall dormers
Round-arched openings
Squat columns

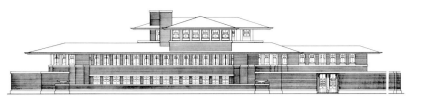

Above: Robie House, Chicago, a landmark in the Prairie Style. (Janis J. Erins, HABS)

Right: Tudor Revival example showing the strong vertical emphasis of decoration and a massive chimney.

Right: Spanish Colonial Revival house with Moorish and medieval details.

Above: Brown-Donahue House, Cape Elizabeth, Maine, a Shingle Style residence. (Gerda Peterich, HABS)

Left: Colonial Revival house emulating characteristics of the Georgian style.

- **Shingle Style (1880–1900)**

General form and interior similar to Queen Anne but more
   horizontal and restrained
Roof and walls covered in wood shingles
Stone foundation
Low tower

- **Beaux Arts (1890–1920)**

Named for the Ecole des Beaux-Arts in Paris
Formal, symmetrical composition
Three-dimensional appearance achieved by projections,
   sculpture and profuse classical ornamentation
Arched windows and doorways
More sedate later examples often called Neoclassical Revival

- **Colonial Revival (1890–1930)**

Formal, rectangular and symmetrical form
Classical features and detailing, usually in the Georgian or
   Federal mode
Primarily in the eastern and northern United States

- **Spanish Colonial Revival (1890–1930)**

Asymmetrical facade
Red tile roof
Arched and flat-topped windows and doorways
Stuccoed walls
Primarily in the Southwest and Florida

- **Tudor Revival (1890–1930)**

Usually asymmetrical in appearance
Steeply pitched gable roof
Decorative half-timbering
Gothic forms and ornamentation
Leaded glass windows
Open floor plan

- **Prairie Style (1900–20)**

Horizontal, low rectangular form
Wide roof overhangs
Brick or wood construction
Open floor plan with central chimney
Examples primarily in the Midwest

■ Late Renaissance Revival (1900–30)

Symmetrical, rectilinear form with horizontal emphasis
Hipped roof, often of ceramic tile
Masonry construction
Round-arched and flat-topped openings
First-floor exterior treated more elaborately than upper
    floor or floors
Less opulent examples, sometimes called Mediterranean:
    simpler ornamentation, a less formal appearance and
    usually stuccoed

■ Craftsman (1900–30)

One-, one-and-a-half- or two-story bungalow type
Horizontal emphasis
Low-pitched gable roof, often with dormers and exposed
    beams
Natural materials, naturally finished
Well-crafted wood trim used judiciously inside and out
Porch supported on tapered piers
Vernacular examples: bungalow forms but lack detail

■ Art Deco (1925–40)

Streamlined form
Modern materials, such as glass block, steel and stucco
Stylized, low-relief ornament not based on historical
    precedents

■ International (1925–50)

Rectangular, rather simple form
Steel, glass and concrete
Horizontal emphasis
Lack of visual reference to historical styles
Total absence of ornament

Horatio Court West Apartments, Santa Monica, Calif., showing elements of the International Style. (S. Westfall, HABS)

OLD-HOUSE TYPES

AND CONSTRUCTION METHODS

Although variations exist, most historic houses are based on one of two types of construction: frame or load-bearing walls. Frame construction is identified by a framework of wood, iron, steel or concrete members arranged horizontally, vertically and sometimes diagonally. These are joined together at their ends to form a sturdy structure. The nonstructural infill is put into place after the framework has been erected. Most wood frame buildings were originally covered with wood siding. During some periods masonry veneers have been used, and stucco has been popular as a facing material for many decades.

Fieldstone I-house and rear wing with sheet-metal roofs. Fieldstone is, simply, stone found in a field. Here it is limestone.

In construction with load-bearing walls, individual bricks, stones, blocks, tiles or other dense materials are arranged one on top of another in a structural configuration to form a sturdy wall. These buildings can be as unpretentious as a fieldstone "half house" or as elaborate as a marble-faced mansion.

A study of American house types can provide important information about the development of a particular house form, its date and location. Certain styles are closely associated with certain house types — for example, wood houses of the Queen Anne and Shingle styles are invariably of balloon-frame construction with a relatively open first floor plan. A knowledge of house types and construction methods is also invaluable in identifying traditional or folk houses, which are most often classified by type. Some of the house types and construction methods are illustrated here and elsewhere in the book.

Wood frame shotgun houses, so named because a shotgun blast fired through the front door would go through the house and out the back door.

Detail of half-timber construction. (David Taylor)

The structural systems of frame houses can be classified a number of ways:

- Heavy timber, mortise-and-tenon frame
- Braced frame, with masonry infill, known as half-timbering, and without masonry infill
- Platform frame, also known as western frame
- Balloon frame
- Iron or steel frame
- Reinforced concrete frame

Above: Brick four-square double house with a hipped roof of slate shingles.

Left: Stuccoed frame bunga-low. (Ohio Historic Preserva-tion Office)

Log house, "discovered," as many are, when its owner began demolition. The log construction has been covered with wood siding as well as a product called Insul-brick. The house rests on a fieldstone foundation.

Load-bearing walls of houses using that type of construction are composed of the following:

- Brick
- Stone
- Adobe
- Block of various types
- Concrete (precast or formed-in-place)
- Sod
- Earth
- Clay tile

By their nature, log houses, not included in either of the above lists, are a cross between both types of construction.

The first houses constructed in the American colonies were functional buildings based loosely on the building traditions of the particular locale from which the settlers came. They were also influenced by the characteristics of the North American region in which they settled. For example, the cold New England climate required central chimneys for heating and cooking, while the warm South permitted locating fireplaces at the end walls. These building traditions continued well into the 19th century and led to the development of various house types suitable to an area and the occupants.

The representative house types listed on the next page are arranged beginning with the earliest type up to the most recent. Most have used both wood frame and load-bearing walls and regional variations and names exist for many.

Side-hall house in Pittsburgh, with a dormer and Italianate motifs.

Historic American House Types

■ **Single room**

Squarish
Gable roof

■ **Double room or hall-and-parlor**

Rectangular with entrance
  to hall space
Gable roof

■ **Center chimney**

Rectangular one- to
  two-story form with
  entrance in center
Gable roof

■ **Side-hall or half house**

Tall, rectangular or
  nearly cubical two-story
  form with entrance at
  side of three-part
  facade
Gable or hipped roof

■ **I-house**

Long, rectangular
  two-story form with
  entrance to hall in center
  of five-part facade
Roof nearly always gable

■ **Four-over-four**

Large, blocklike two-story
  form, two rooms deep
  with entrance to hall
  in center of five-part
  facade
Gable, hipped or gambrel
  roof, low to high pitch

■ **Shotgun**

Long, rectangular one-
  story form with facade
  at short side
Gable or hipped roof,
  facing front

■ **Octagon**

Eight-sided, one- or two-
  story form
Hipped roof

■ **Row**

Long, rectangular,
  one- to three-story
  form, multiple dwelling
  with party walls
  separating the units
  and each unit often a
  side-hall type
Gable, hipped, gambrel
  or mansard roof

■ **Gable ell**

Ell-shaped two-story form
  with a porch in the
  enclosed space and the
  facade at the short or
  long side
Gable roof

■ **Open plan**

Irregular variation of
  gable ell type with
  two- or three-story
  form, often with
  tower
Complex gable and hipped
  roof or mansard roof

■ **Four-square**

Squarish or cubical,
  two- or two-and-a-
  half-story
  single or double
  residence with porch
  across facade
Front-facing gable or
  hipped roof with
  dormers

■ **Bungalow**

Low, rectangular one-
  or two-story form with
  porch
Low gable roof with
  dormers

■ **Ranch**

Rectangular, one-story
  form
Low gable or hipped
  roof

■ **Split-level**

Rectangular, low two-story
  form with center
  entrance
Usually two gable or
  hipped roofs

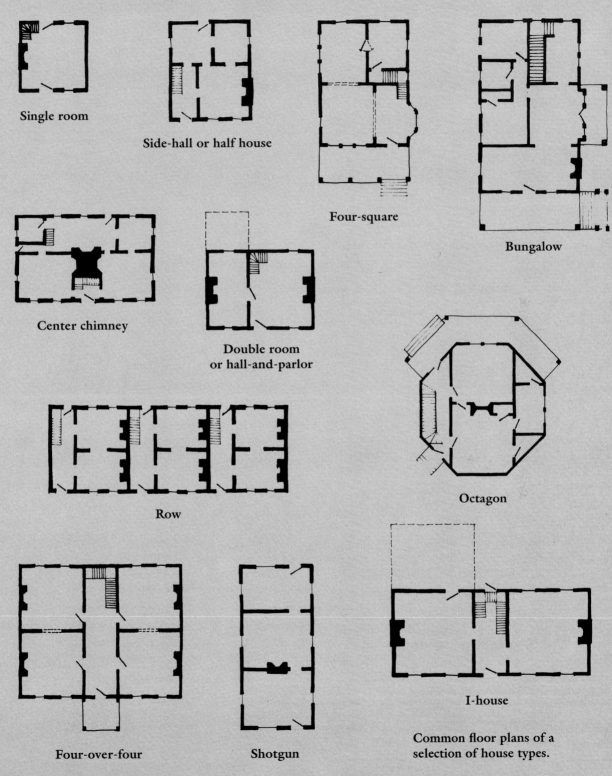

Single room

Side-hall or half house

Four-square

Bungalow

Center chimney

Double room
or hall-and-parlor

Octagon

Row

Four-over-four

Shotgun

I-house

Common floor plans of a
selection of house types.

Roof combs or cresting

Double-hung windows,
one-over-one with fixed transom

Modified Palladian window

Gable
slate roof

Round tower
with conical roof

Round arch
opening to
recessed porch

Gutter

Attic vent

Finial

Round
dormer

Eaves

Wood-shingle
siding

Wrap around
porch supported
on columns

Triangular pediment

Balustrade

Downspout

RESEARCHING THE OLD HOUSE

The best source of information about your old house is always the house itself. Similarly, information about the history of the site, including outbuildings, landscaping and other features, is available mainly from the site. Almost without exception, evidence of original features and finishes can be found underneath later work. Often such information as the original exterior colors can be discovered by exposing the layers of paint that have accumulated over the years in areas not subject to weathering or not exposed to direct sunlight. Also, the physical evidence present in the house can be used to confirm or refute information found in written and oral sources. Consider conducting some physical research while inspecting the house to assess its condition (see page 109).

The object is to ascertain as much information as possible about the historic appearance of the house and what visual changes have been made in the years since it was built. The study may be for information purposes only. If you have found that you like all of its modern conveniences, you will have no intention of restoring the house to its original appearance and condition. However, you may want to rehabilitate it — for example, restore the original ornate porch

Opposite: Balloon-framed Queen Anne house in an open plan with neoclassical elements.

Urban archeology in Cincinnati's Betts-Longworth Historic District. This unusual beehive cistern was discovered under the foundation of a later building, which had been covered by a brick patio and a concrete walkway. (Miami Purchase Association)

railing, pieces of which are now missing, or remove a temporary partition from the second floor. To find answers to your questions, you will need to do some physical research and possibly some research using written and oral primary sources. You may want to have a historic structure report prepared for the house (see page 125). This report includes all the historical data, plus a detailed assessment of the current condition of the house, and it covers all work that needs to be done.

INVESTIGATING THE SITE

Research on the building's site can be very rewarding, particularly if you are trying to determine the location and appearance of historic but vanished structures or other features, such as walkways, arbors, walls, cisterns, drains, wells and trash pits. It is absolutely essential that you get advice from a professional archeologist. The danger of a do-it-yourself approach is that you will not know or be able to interpret what you have found and may inadvertently destroy important evidence or dig up the whole site unnecessarily. The potential value of archeological research for any old house cannot be underestimated. Rarely will a historic house site fail to yield important data.

INVESTIGATING THE EXTERIOR

You may first want to look for signs of additions to the original building. Occasionally researchers discover that what everyone assumed was the core of the original building is actually a later, more pretentious addition to a simple early structure. Keep your eyes and mind open to physical clues, such as subtle changes in the type or color of masonry, siding that does not match or line up exactly, a change in the window pattern, or indications (usually most evident in the attic) that the roof has been altered. Such scientific techniques as how the wood is sawn, wood joinery methods, nail chronology and dendrochronology (wood dating) will be helpful in some cases.

You may also want to determine whether or not the

windows are the originals, what the original roofing material was or any number of facts about the exterior appearance of the house.

INVESTIGATING THE INTERIOR

Look initially for obvious changes to the floor plan. Look for walls that are not the same thickness as other walls of their type (either structural or nonstructural), a change in materials (from plaster to plasterboard, for example) or an awkward partition. Knowledge of floor plans typical for the house type you are dealing with is beneficial.

Some common changes will be obvious to you — lowered ceilings, newer sections of wood flooring, evidence of removed walls or nonoriginal cabinets — while others may be more subtle. Some houses have been so cleverly and thoroughly altered over the years that they defy anyone to determine the original floor plan, wall finishes or hardware. If you are not going to restore the interior, you may decide that the investigation is not worth the effort. On the other hand, you may wish to hire a professional trained in the area of historic interiors to assist in your research effort.

USING WRITTEN AND ORAL SOURCES

Before planning any project, you will want to find out as much as you can about the history of your old house. This can be a very rewarding experience, and it often leads to some fascinating discoveries. The effort can also be tedious, time consuming and produce little useful information, although this result is the exception rather than the rule.

Primary source material in this research effort is original information spoken or written by people who actually experienced or witnessed the events contained in the account. The information has not been taken, derived or interpreted from any other source. Secondary source material is oral and written information that has been copied, derived, or interpreted from primary or other sources. If the source is a compilation of information, chances are that it is a secondary source.

If you have not done historical research before, you will

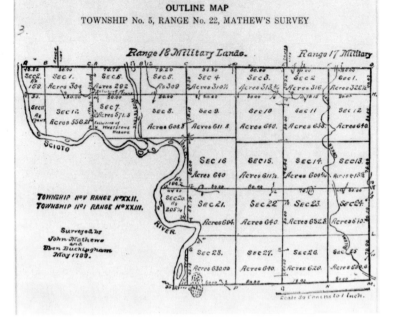

OUTLINE MAP
TOWNSHIP No. 5, RANGE No. 22, MATHEW'S SURVEY

Historic map of a land sale
found in a property abstract
for a Columbus, Ohio, house.

need to acquaint yourself with libraries and collections that may have materials helpful to you. Nothing is more frustrating than a day spent at a library that, as it turns out, has no information useful for your research work! Telephone calls to the nearest library and the village, city, county or state historical society are the most efficient way to begin your research.

Use as much primary source material as you can reasonably find. You may need to look at several secondary sources, such as state historic inventory forms or town or county histories to start the research effort. These sources can provide such basic data as the building's style and its approximate date, who settled the area and when, and so forth. Also, they can give you clues as to the next steps to take in your research effort, such as which primary source materials might be available and helpful for researching your house. If the house is located in a community that has city directories, you may want to trace back as far as you can to determine who occupied the house at a particular date. This knowledge will give you a place to start more detailed research.

A trip to the office of the recorder of deeds is nearly al-

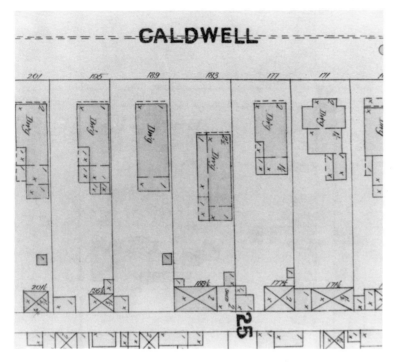

Section of a Sanborn insurance map for a residential area in a small town, 1890. Note that building outlines, street addresses and dimensions are given. Construction materials are indicated by color—pink for brick, gray for stone and yellow for wood frame. (Sanborn Perris Map Company, New York)

ways essential, unless you have located a property abstract, which will include the history of ownership of the property. Work backward from the current owner to the earlier owners. A deed may disclose an "improvement" to the land, meaning that a structure was built. Also, a sharp increase in the price paid for land may indicate that a house was constructed on it by the seller. Tax records provide similar information regarding increases in property value.

You may not be able to use a primary source because it does not exist, or you may find conflicting information. If so, remember that each conclusion you reach — regarding the year the house was built, who built it, when additions were made or anything else — should be substantiated by at least two sources. Interviews can be extremely valuable sources of primary information. Remember, too, that one of your sources can be the physical evidence present in the house itself.

Be sure to have a copy of your research work available for the next owner of the house, and provide a copy to your local or state historical society and library for its archives. Remember that the information you have laboriously gathered can be immensely useful to others, too!

Primary Sources for Researching Historic Houses

- Property abstracts, compilations of information about the sequence of ownership of the property taken from deed and other public records, which the previous owner may have

- Deed records at the local (usually the county) recorder's office

- Tax records at the local (usually the county) treasurer's office

- Census records

- Marriage records

- Death records

- Interviews, particularly with the current and previous owners and with people who lived in the house at one time or were involved in its design and construction

- City directories for finding out when the house was constructed and who occupied it

- Maps of all types (check with community and county offices), particularly insurance maps, such as those issued by the Sanborn Map Company of New York

- Subdivision and plat books

- Atlases

- Photographs

- Lithographs and prints

- Personal property inventories

- Wills and probate records

- Letters and other correspondence, such as greeting cards, announcements and postcards from visiting family members and friends

- Family papers, including financial and personal records

- Scrapbooks

- Insurance records

- Land surveys

- Building permits

- Architectural, engineering and contractors' drawings, specifications and records of transactions

- Builders' guides and other similar books for help in locating specific details and building features

- Obituaries and news items in newspapers

- Newspaper and magazine articles on building design, styles and construction techniques

- Catalogs, including those for entire houses, specific building materials, products and furnishings

Above left: James Thurber House, a Princess Anne residence in Columbus, Ohio, at the turn of the century. Historic photographs such as this are of enormous help in any rehabilitation effort. (The Thurber House)

Above right: The Thurber House in 1983, before rehabilitation. (Kathy Mast Kane)

Left: The Thurber House today, showing rehabilitated exterior including the reconstructed porch and newly installed beveled glass.

SAFEGUARDING PROPERTIES

Taking care of a property, especially when that property is old, can mean much more than simply repainting wood and repairing cracks in plaster. Here are the first six procedures you can follow to preserve a house before beginning any actual physical work. These approaches do not involve construction and are recommended to ensure that actual construction work, which comes later, will be effective and sensitive to the building's historical attributes.

IDENTIFICATION

Identification is the most basic preservation task; without it, no planning can be done. The heart of any preservation effort is knowing what is worthy of preservation. Identification of historic properties most often occurs as a result of a geographical survey, which is confined to a distinct area. It usually is funded locally or by the state historic preservation agency through state or federal funds in order to locate and research the historic properties within the survey area.

Thematic surveys do exist, but they are expensive and time consuming to conduct. They are most common for certain easily identifiable resources, such as bridges of various types or the works of a well-known architect in a particular city. The best-known thematic survey is the ongoing Historic Sites Survey of the National Park Service, whose purpose is to identify and research properties of national significance that are eligible for designation as National Historic Landmarks.

Geographical surveys are the type with which most peo-

Above: Volunteers, during a summer survey, studying porch paint on a house benefiting from a revolving fund. (Historic Kansas City Foundation)

Opposite: Shingled houses in Nantucket, Mass., where residents have united to prevent overdevelopment of the fragile island. (Jack Boucher, HABS)

OHIO HISTORIC INVENTORY

Ohio Historic Preservation Office
1985 Velma Avenue
Columbus, Ohio 43211
614/297-2470

OHIO HISTORICAL SOCIETY
SINCE 1885

1. No.	2. County	4. Present Name(s)		
			☐ Coded	
3. Location of Negatives		5. Historic or Other Name(s)		
Roll No. Picture No.(s)				

6. Specific Address or Location	16. Thematic Association(s)	28. No. of Stories
		29. Basement? Yes ☐
		No ☐
6a. Lot, Section or VMD Number	17. Date(s) or Period / 17b. Alteration Date(s)	30. Foundation Material
	18. Style or Design ☐ High Style ☐ Elements	31. Wall Construction
7. City or Village If Rural, Township & Vicinity	18a. Style of Addition or Element(s)	
		32. Roof Type & Material
8. Site Plan with North Arrow	19. Architect or Engineer	
		33. No. of Bays
	19a. Design Sources	Front Side
		34. Exterior Wall Material(s)
	20. Contractor or Builder	
		35. Plan Shape
	21. Building Type or Plan	36. Changes Addition ☐
		(Explain Altered ☐
	22. Original Use, if apparent	in #42) Moved ☐
		37. Window Type(s)
9. U.T.M. Reference	23. Present Use	☐ 6 over 6 ☐ 2 over 2
Quadrangle Name		☐ 4 over 4 ☐ Other
Zone Easting Northing	24. Ownership Public ☐	38. Building Dimensions
10. Site ☐ Structure ☐	Private ☐	39. Endangered? Yes ☐
Building ☐ Object ☐	25. Owner's Name & Address, if known	By What? No ☐
11. On National Yes ☐ 12. N.R. Yes ☐		
Register? No ☐ Potential? No ☐		40. Chimney Placement
13. Part of Estab. Yes ☐ 14. District Yes ☐		
Hist. Dist.? No ☐ Potential? No ☐	26. Property Acreage	41. Distance from and
15. Name of Established District (N.R. or Local)	27. Other Surveys in Which Included	Frontage on Road

42. Further Description of Important Interior and Exterior Features (Continue on reverse if necessary)

PHOTO

43. History and Significance (Continue on reverse if necessary)

PHOTO

44. Description of Environment and Outbuildings (See #52)

46. Prepared by
47. Organization
48. Date Recorded in Field

45. Sources of Information

49. Revised by	50a. Date Revised
50b. Reviewed by	

(Right margin tabs: 1. No. | 2. County | 4,5. Present or Historic Name | 6. Specific Address or Location)

64

Opposite: First page of a state inventory form used to survey historic houses.

Left: Conducting a survey of structures in Landsdowne, Md. Such geographical surveys require much time and personal effort to ensure accuracy. (Maryland Historical Trust)

ple are familiar. These are often conducted by a professional consultant or by groups of volunteers or students under the direction of an experienced leader or teacher. Homeowners associations have produced some of the best and most thorough survey results, or inventories, in the country and have published pamphlets or books on the history of a particular county, community or neighborhood, and its houses.

Inventory forms are generally streamlined, rarely more

than a few pages in length and often just a single page. Here is the place to use the research information you have gathered about your house. The information required is usually related more to the physical appearance and condition of the building than to in-depth historical research data. The forms are available from your state historic preservation office or local preservation official. Since you will want your work to be recorded in the state and local data banks of inventory information, it is a good idea to use existing forms developed for the purpose rather than designing your own. Any specific data you are collecting can easily be gathered as an addendum to your state's standard inventory form.

LISTING

Including a property in the national or a local list of significant historic structures is not a guarantee of preservation but does help to label the property as an important part of the country's or community's architectural and cultural resources. While it may not be tangible, this "prestige value" alone can be a significant preservation tool.

Listing or landmark designation can occur at the national level, at the state level and at the local (village, city, township or county) level. Cultural resources of global significance are included in the World Heritage List, published by the U.S. Committee, International Council on Monuments and Sites.

NATIONAL LISTING

The National Historic Landmark designation, first begun in 1935, is the highest distinction the federal government can give to a property. It means that the property has been determined to have archeological, historical or architectural significance to the nation as a whole. Properties are considered for National Historic Landmark status after extensive research and approval by the National Park Service. Many nationally significant houses and residential areas are National Historic Landmarks.

The National Register of Historic Places was created by the National Historic Preservation Act of 1966 and began with a core of listings — the previously designated National Historic Landmark properties. National Register nominations are received from the states or, in the case of federally owned property, from a federal agency. Unlike National Historic Landmarks, properties eligible for the National Register of Historic Places can be significant at the state or local level (see the National Register criteria on page 73).

The nomination form requires detailed information about the location and ownership of the property, a complete description of interior and exterior architectural features, a description of the site, a succinct statement of why the property meets the National Register criteria and historical data appropriate to the property being nominated. While the National Register nomination form is not designed to include all information available about every property, this is the place to use the data you have gathered

Workers' housing, Springfield, Ohio. Along with the early industrial complex around which this neighborhood grew, these houses are being considered for nomination to the National Register. (Jeffrey T. Darbee)

OMB No. 1024-0018

United States Department of the Interior
National Park Service

National Register of Historic Places
Registration Form

This form is for use in nominating or requesting determinations of eligibility for individual properties or districts. See instructions in *Guidelines for Completing National Register Forms* (National Register Bulletin 16). Complete each item by marking ''x'' in the appropriate box or by entering the requested information. If an item does not apply to the property being documented, enter ''N/A'' for ''not applicable.'' For functions, styles, materials, and areas of significance, enter only the categories and subcategories listed in the instructions. For additional space use continuation sheets (Form 10-900a). Type all entries.

1. Name of Property

historic name _____

other names/site number _____

2. Location

street & number _____ ☐ not for publication

city, town _____ ☐ vicinity

state _____ code _____ county _____ code _____ zip code _____

3. Classification

Ownership of Property
☐ private
☐ public-local
☐ public-State
☐ public-Federal

Category of Property
☐ building(s)
☐ district
☐ site
☐ structure
☐ object

Number of Resources within Property

Contributing	Noncontributing	
_____	_____	buildings
_____	_____	sites
_____	_____	structures
_____	_____	objects
_____	_____	Total

Name of related multiple property listing:

_____

Number of contributing resources previously listed in the National Register _____

4. State/Federal Agency Certification

As the designated authority under the National Historic Preservation Act of 1966, as amended, I hereby certify that this ☐ nomination ☐ request for determination of eligibility meets the documentation standards for registering properties in the National Register of Historic Places and meets the procedural and professional requirements set forth in 36 CFR Part 60. In my opinion, the property ☐ meets ☐ does not meet the National Register criteria. ☐ See continuation sheet.

Signature of certifying official _____ Date _____

State or Federal agency and bureau _____

In my opinion, the property ☐ meets ☐ does not meet the National Register criteria. ☐ See continuation sheet.

Signature of commenting or other official _____ Date _____

State or Federal agency and bureau _____

5. National Park Service Certification

I, hereby, certify that this property is:

☐ entered in the National Register.
   ☐ See continuation sheet.
☐ determined eligible for the National
   Register. ☐ See continuation sheet.
☐ determined not eligible for the
   National Register.

☐ removed from the National Register.
☐ other, (explain:) _____

_____

_____ _____
Signature of the Keeper   Date of Action

from the physical study of the building and its site and from written and oral sources. The nomination must also include high-quality photographs.

The completed nomination is submitted to the state historic preservation office, where it is reviewed by the professional staff. If approved, it is scheduled for consideration by a state review board, which determines whether the site, building or historic district being nominated appears to meet the National Register criteria. This phase of the listing process can take some time, since most review boards meet only a few times each year. Following approval by the state board, the nomination is signed by the state historic preservation officer and forwarded to the National Park Service in Washington, D.C., for final review and listing.

If at the time the nomination is made the owner objects to the property's listing or if a majority of owners of property in a nominated historic district object, the property will not be listed. Regrettably, the consequences of National Register listing are often misunderstood. Property owners retain all rights of ownership and may do what they wish with the property, including demolishing it.

Before releasing funds or issuing a permit for a project, federal entities, such as the Department of Housing and Urban Development, must assess the impact of any funding on the properties listed in or eligible for listing in the National Register. The state historic preservation offices and the Advisory Council on Historic Preservation in Washington, D.C., are also participants in this review process.

One tangible benefit of National Register listing is that the property owner is eligible for 50 percent federal matching grants, administered by the state historic preservation offices, for rehabilitation and restoration work. Although such funds have not been available in recent years, they are currently being made available again in very limited amounts.

Another benefit, for income-producing properties only, including rental housing, is eligibility for a federal tax credit for qualified rehabilitation work to the building.

The National Register nomination form and further advice regarding its preparation are available from each state historic preservation office. The form is an important and rather complex document, and its preparation should not be taken lightly. It definitely cannot be completed in one evening!

Opposite: First page of the National Register of Historic Places nomination form.

STATE LISTING

A majority of states have registers, some of these state versions of the National Register of Historic Places, with similar reviews of state-funded projects and benefits. Others are quite different. Your state historic preservation office will be able to assist you with any questions.

Some states recognize historic homesteads as historic sites. These are generally properties that have been owned by the same family for 100 years or more. While this is not considered a historic preservation program, because recognition is based on land ownership rather than on the significance of historic houses or other structures, the information provided can be of help in historic preservation research.

LOCAL LISTING

Since local landmarks legislation can provide by far the most protection for historic houses through local review of proposed changes to properties, the local listing process is of enormous importance to the cause of historic preservation in the United States. Of course, some local listings provide recognition only — the owner receives a plaque or marker for the building, along with a certificate — but no design review follow-up and, hence, no real protection for the property (see Zoning, below).

ZONING

Since the National Register of Historic Places and most state registers provide only limited protection for landmarks and historic districts, the bulk of protection for historic properties exists at the local level through special zoning for those properties listed as landmarks and historic districts in local registers. Proposed changes to these listed properties are reviewed by landmarks commissions or design review boards set up by a zoning ordinance and made up of interested individuals usually appointed by the mayor. (see Local Design Review on page 83.)

ACQUISITION

Acquisition of a historic house itself as well as acquisitions of facade and open-space easements can be powerful tools in ensuring the preservation of the house and its significant features.

An easement is partial ownership or control of a prop-

Morris Marks residence, Portland, Ore. In this unusual case, rezoning from residential to commercial prevented the house from becoming a series of apartments thus destroying the interior. A law firm moved its offices into the residence. (Oregon Historical Society)

Common Burying Ground and Island Cemetery, Newport, R.I., listed in the National Register because of its historical importance to the area and the nation.

erty. A power company may purchase an easement to a strip of land running across farm fields in order to extend its transmission lines, now or at some future date. In the same way, a historic preservation organization may hold an easement to a historic property donated by a sympathetic owner to protect the property from harm by others, now or into the future. In this case the organization is likely to be in existence long after the owner dies.

A facade easement is generally desirable if the property is a town house, while an open-space easement will protect

CRITERIA FOR THE NATIONAL REGISTER OF HISTORIC PLACES

The following criteria are designed to guide the states, federal agencies and the secretary of the U.S. Department of the Interior in evaluating potential entries (other than areas of the National Park System and National Historic Landmarks) for the National Register:

The quality of significance in American history, architecture, archeology and culture is present in districts, sites, buildings, structures and objects that possess integrity of location, design, setting, materials, workmanship, feeling and association, and:

A. That are associated with events that have made a significant contribution to the broad patterns of our history; or

B. That are associated with the lives of persons significant in our past; or

C. That embody the distinctive characteristics of a type, period or method of construction, or that represent the work of a master, or that possess high artistic values, or that represent a significant and distinguishable entity whose components may lack individual distinction; or

D. That have yielded, or may be likely to yield, information important in prehistory or history.

Ordinarily cemeteries, birthplaces or graves of historical figures, properties owned by religious institutions or used for religious purposes, structures that have been moved from their original locations, reconstructed historic buildings, properties primarily commemorative in nature and properties that have achieved significance within the past 50 years shall not be considered eligible for the National Register. However, such properties will qualify if they are integral parts of districts that do meet the criteria or if they fall within the following categories:

- Religious property deriving primary significance from architectural or artistic distinction or historical importance; or

- Building or structure removed from its original location but which is significant primarily for architectural value, or which is the surviving structure most importantly associated with a historic person or event; or

- Birthplace or grave of a historical figure of outstanding importance if there is no other appropriate site or building directly associated with that figure's productive life; or

- Cemetery that derives its primary significance from graves of persons of transcendent importance, from age, from distinctive design features or from association with historic events; or

- Reconstructed building when accurately executed in a suitable environment and presented in a dignified manner as part of a restoration master plan and when no other building or structure with the same association has survived; or

- Property primarily commemorative in intent if design, age, tradition or symbolic value has invested it with its own historical significance; or

- Property achieving significance within the past 50 years if it is of exceptional importance.

the area surrounding a suburban or rural property from inappropriate development, thereby preserving the historic setting of the house. Easements are generally donated in perpetuity to a qualifying village, city or state government or not-for-profit organization, enabling the property owner to claim the value of the easement as a charitable deduction on income taxes. In order to qualify, the property must be individually listed in the National Register of Historic Places or be certified by the National Park Service as contributing to the significance of a National Register–listed historic district.

Another acquisition technique, popular in cities where buildable land is in short supply, is the transfer of development rights (TDR), which entails the sale of building rights not being used by the owner of the historic property (called air rights) to another owner, who can use these rights to construct a larger building than would otherwise be possible on another site. If a city has such a development rights transfer program, it also will have specific sites or zones designated as areas where these rights can be used.

Farmhouse for which an open-space easement would be appropriate, and perhaps essential, to safeguard its rural setting. (Ohio Historic Preservation Office)

Town house in a historic district. The owner donated a facade easement to the city, which funded the rehabilitation of the facade with the help of local and federal funds and the community's historic preservation organization. (Ohio Historic Preservation Office)

Documentation

Professional-quality measured drawings and photographs of a house can be essential to its preservation if it is damaged by fire, hurricane, earthquake or tornado. The Historic American Buildings Survey of the National Park Service has established standards for the preparation of such materials. Such documentation is particularly important for unusual structures or museum buildings, and it may be required by some insurance companies before they will agree to insure houses with unusual, unique or particularly valuable architectural features.

Marking

Identifying a property or area of properties with distinctive signs is a significant step toward the recognition and, therefore, the preservation of the historic aspects of houses and the neighborhood. As an alternative to marking each building, sometimes just the boundaries of the neighborhood are indicated by a sign at each major pedestrian and vehicular entrance. A self-guided walking tour can be promoted by signs placed in the area.

National Register marker on an individually listed historic house. A number of companies offer these bronze plaques for sale to National Register property owners. Historic neighborhood associations often have their own markers designed and produced, some of them personalized for each house.

THIS PROPERTY HAS BEEN PLACED ON THE NATIONAL REGISTER OF HISTORIC PLACES BY THE UNITED STATES DEPARTMENT OF THE INTERIOR

ASSOCIATIONS CAN DO

Following are several steps that can be taken by a group of individuals to help set a preservation agenda for the community.

■ Ask for volunteers and information. The volunteers can do everything from photographing buildings for the survey to organizing fund-raising events. The information is needed for the historical research effort.

■ Complete a basic history of the area and a comprehensive survey of its buildings; the result will be a written body of well-organized inventory information. All the historic houses and other buildings, including barns, garages and other ancillary structures, should be researched and recorded. Of particular importance are high-quality photographs and maps.

■ Publish the research results in an easily available form, such as a booklet or pamphlet that can be distributed free or at nominal cost. Do not hesitate to publish something before the comprehensive inventory is finished. The publication could attract funding so the inventory can be com-

Books on design guidelines produced by and for specific communities and historic districts, homeowners and design review commissions. Such books are of vital importance in educating and informing property owners, real estate agents and the general public about what is and is not appropriate for houses and other historic buildings in the area.

pleted. A walking tour has worked well in a number of communities. The idea is to get the word out about the area's historic and visual significance and its potential for preservation. Another effective way to publicize the area may be through a series of newspaper articles.

- Focus on people as well as on architecture in your research efforts. Interest in an area will increase if information about the people who settled there, built the buildings and lived in them is an integral part of the written material. Perhaps a manufacturer who started a major company grew up in the area, a restaurant on the corner was an important gathering place for workers or an influential local organization got its start in one of the houses.

- Place markers at the boundaries of the neighborhood so that motorists and pedestrians will know its exact location. Consider involving real estate professionals in this effort.

- Find out what the property owners and residents want in addition to preservation. A good way to approach this is a series of neighborhood forums, which also have the benefit of introducing neighbors to one another.

- Develop a display to use in an appropriate place or as part of an appropriate event. A display at the city hall, county fair or local arts festival, for example, could be quite effective in spreading information about the historic neighborhood. The display could consist simply of a series of mounted photographs, a sign identifying the neighborhood and, perhaps, pamphlets.

- Sponsor an event in the neighborhood to get people to come see for themselves how nice it is. This event could coincide with National Historic Preservation Week, which is always the second week in May. Sponsor a special tour of the houses or gardens, a holiday tour or a theme tour highlighting the work of a particular architect or craftsperson. Consider hosting a block party to which key officials are invited. Have a village or city council meeting in the neighborhood.

- Invite an expert from another area (more than 50 miles away) to assess the significance of the neighborhood and give an objective opinion on its eligibility for listing in the National Register of Historic Places. This effort may qualify your organization for a grant. Although by that time local experts will have given you some idea as to whether or

WHAT COMMUNITY OR NEIGHBORHOOD

Neighborhood fair in Portland, Ore. Such events can mean a boost for a community but can also have a negative impact.

not the area qualifies for listing, the opinion of the out-of-town authority is essential because, of course, this person will have no financial or other special interest in the future of the area.

■ Nominate the historic district or a series of individual houses to the National Register of Historic Places. The advice of the state historic preservation office will be needed.

■ Plan and work toward local protection for historic buildings. This generally means promulgating a local ordinance that provides for mandatory review of any proposed changes to the neighborhood by a landmarks commission or design review board. Homework is necessary here. By now, through contact with various local experts, your state historic preservation officer and others, you should be familiar with the activities, both successful and unsuccessful, of communities similar to yours in size, location, economic base and other significant factors. Study what these cities and villages have done. (See Local Design Review, page 83.)

■ Develop a financial strategy for both economic and physical revitalization. Your direction will depend a great deal on the nature of the neighborhood, the condition of the buildings and their uses. The goal is to assist both long-time and new owners and residents with the tasks of purchasing, preserving and rehabilitating.

■ Maintain lists of contractors and craftspersons gathered from the experiences of neighborhood residents. Lists of materials suppliers, such as sources of old slate and bricks for repairs, are helpful as well.

■ Establish neighborhood programs to assist residents, such as a babysitting cooperative, a friends program for the elderly and homebound and a neighborhood block-watch program to deter crime. Be mindful of the needs of all the neighbors.

■ Organize activities for the residents of the neighborhood, such as a weekly or monthly newsletter, performances in the park, "dollars-off" at local businesses, a group picture, a party or a parade. Such activities will show that those who have believed in the area and invested their time, energy and money in its revitalization have not been forgotten in the effort to publicize the neighborhood. Success has a price, unfortunately, and the neighborhood may suddenly seem to exist primarily for those who visit rather than those

Opposite: Tour of a neighborhood in Vermont. Such tours help to establish a neighborhood as a viable part of the area's cultural past. (Philip C. Marshall)

who live there. The residential-commercial balance is very fragile in most historic neighborhoods and requires a tremendous amount of energy to maintain.

■ Assist the design review board or landmarks commission in any way possible, such as by helping to establish architectural guidelines for work in the historic district, researching difficult issues that the board or commission faces or aiding in a crisis, such as a fire or natural disaster that threatens buildings in the district. Other threats may come from businesses or institutions — colleges or universities, hospitals, churches, industries or banks that may wish to demolish neighborhood buildings or convert them to nonresidential use as part of an expansion plan.

■ Share your successes and experience with other neighborhood associations in your area and elsewhere. Remember the help and encouragement you got from others!

ORGANIZING A SUCCESSFUL

GRASS-ROOTS CAMPAIGN

Now that you've read about the six best ways to safeguard a property, there are key steps you can take to establish a winning strategy in saving a historic house or other architectural or cultural resource. You will integrate those six safeguards — identification, listing, zoning, acquisition, documentation and marking — throughout your organizing effort.

Organize your preservation group carefully and effectively. If your group is an existing one with general goals, you may want to consider creating an affiliated but separate entity to handle a specific preservation campaign. A prolonged battle may drain support, energy and funding away from the parent organization. You may prefer to create a new organization just to carry out the goal of preserving a specific house or houses.

Find and organize behind effective leadership. Often the people best suited to lead the effort are those who are not primarily associated with historic preservation in the community.

LOCAL DESIGN REVIEW: A DOZEN WAYS TO MAKE IT EFFECTIVE

1. An ordinance establishing a landmarks commission or design review board should, at a minimum, include the following:

- Statement of purpose

- List of definitions of terms, such as "historic district," "listed property," "alteration," which appear in the ordinance

- Procedures for establishing a landmarks commission or design review board

- List of powers and responsibilities of the commission or board

- Criteria and procedures for identifying, reviewing and designating individual landmarks and historic districts

- Procedures for reviewing and approving proposed alterations to designated resources, including relocation, demolition and new construction

- Enforcement provisions and penalties

- Minimum maintenance requirement (to prevent an owner from effectively demolishing a building by neglecting it)

- Procedures for appeals

2. The commission or board should be made up of individuals who have a demonstrated interest in historic preservation.

3. Staff assistance to the commission or board should be provided by the governing authority.

4. Commission or board meetings should be held frequently enough to avoid waits of more than six weeks for applicants.

5. Criteria for selection of potential landmarks and historic districts should be broad enough to include properties significant in the areas of archeology, history and architecture.

6. Review should apply equally to all property owners, public and private, commercial and noncommercial, for-profit and not-for-profit.

7. Review must be mandatory, covering, at a minimum, all exterior alterations to properties, including relocation, demolition and new construction.

8. Consideration should be given to review of proposed work to significant interiors.

9. The landmarks commission or design review board must, following the designation of a landmark or historic district, oversee the development and distribution of specific design guidelines, which it will use to review proposed alterations and new construction.

10. The commission or board should work toward educating and informing the citizens of the community about historic preservation.

11. The board or commission should review its legislation and rules of procedure periodically and make recommendations for necessary changes.

12. The commission or board should have the general support of community officials and be well integrated into the local governmental structure.

Laundon House, Elyria, Ohio, preserved through the efforts of the Lorain County Historical Society, including challenging the will of the owner, who wanted the house demolished upon her death. The house is now being rehabilitated by a private owner.

Establish a streamlined decision-making system that allows for quick action, should events warrant it.

Broaden your base of support as much as you can. You may find allies in unexpected places.

Negotiate for more time when dealing with adversarial parties for you will need it to do the other things on this list.

Develop well-thought-out alternatives to demolition, and be firm but not so rigid that you reject reasonable compromises.

Educate the public, if appropriate, to help foster awareness of what you are trying to do.

Get advice from recognized experts. If an appraisal of a historic property is needed, for example, go to someone who has expertise in this specific area. If a financial feasibility study is needed, offer to pay for it.

Advertise in appropriate publications, such as the *Wall Street Journal* or *Historic Preservation News,* the newspaper of the National Trust for Historic Preservation, to find an interested and qualified developer. Don't assume that no one outside your community is interested in the property.

Build community support and credibility for your organization and your goal. Do not use emotional arguments as your main strategy.

Publicize your successes effectively and appropriately.

Establish a cordial relationship with your opposition, if at all possible. Assume that you are dealing with reasonable people who have no hidden agenda. Existing relationships are useful, and one-on-one contacts are quite effective. Be aware of the political ramifications of the situation.

Recognize the possibility that the other side may have some very good suggestions. Be firm in your resolve, but keep an open mind. And, by all means, listen to everyone. Do not think in terms of "winners" and "losers." If there is a way for the opposition to come out of the controversy looking good while you achieve your objectives, then by all means move in that direction.

Move quickly to disprove incorrect or invalid information.

Keep the lines of communication open at all times.

Realize that it may be appropriate to put the issue to a communitywide or countywide vote, as in the case of a publicly owned house or one for which a public use has been proposed. Again, stick to the issue at hand and resist the temptation to make the other side look bad. Concentrate instead on giving the public factual information. Sound financial data will be read and remembered.

HOW MUCH WILL IT COST?

Residential real estate for the most part is an excellent investment, whether the property is a house that you and your family occupy or one that you rent to tenants. Money wisely invested in the purchase and rehabilitation of most real property has for many years earned a healthy return. Historical real estate investments, while not free of risk, nearly always appreciate in value, particularly when the properties are rehabilitated as part of a neighborhood physical and economic revitalization effort.

Much more financial information is available today about the real cost of historic preservation work than was known only a few years ago, primarily because of numerous recent studies of projects qualifying for federal rehabilitation tax credits. Through the practical experience of federal, state and local preservation organizations, along with the actual financial information given in trade publications by architects, contractors and materials suppliers, the cost of individual aspects of a historic preservation effort often can be predicted with a great deal of accuracy. Of course, each house is unique and each project has unanticipated problems, but even items such as structural work needed to stabilize a fire-damaged wall or weakened foundation or necessary improvements to the condition of an enclosed water drainage system can be reliably assessed. Chances are good that for any problem the results of at least one comparable study will be available.

Obviously money is an important consideration, whether you are rehabilitating a house for yourself or converting a historic residence for retail or office use. You will want to have a reasonable estimate of what the overall project is likely to cost before you agree to purchase the house. A

Above: Gable ell house in Louisville, Ky., acquired and rehabilitated through a revolving fund and then resold to private owners. (Preservation Alliance)

Opposite: San Francisco Victorian getting a new coat of paint. (Lee Foster)

lender or partner also will need this information.

Since very few of us can afford to move ahead with rehabilitation work without first establishing a budget for the project and since a careful, well-planned approach is a "must" no matter how much money you have, you will need to do your homework. Friends or relatives may tell you that their projects cost two to three times what they had originally estimated, that the contractors they hired worked diligently for a week and then disappeared for a month, or that the results were not at all what they anticipated. These tales of woe indicate poor planning, which can lead to serious mistakes, wasted time and money and irreversible damage to the historic house. Your estimate should be reliable. It must be something you can count on.

While your bill for redecorating a couple of rooms may total only a few hundred dollars, it is likely that the house will need more than this. How much this work will cost varies from building to building and from region to region. The most sensible approach is to determine by thorough study the work needed to make the house livable and safe and combine this appraisal with your particular desires. The basic work, from roof repair to electrical work, should always come first. The temptation to wallpaper the living room next may be very strong, for example, but wait until the springy floors upstairs are investigated and properly repaired.

Many architects and contractors will speak of per-square-foot costs. Understandably, the statement, "Well, it will run you about $20 to $45 per square foot to rehabilitate the house, depending upon what we find," is not the kind of specific data that the bank — or you — had in mind when you asked for an estimate. An estimate that breaks the work down into understandable components is essential. Insist on it.

One way to approach the estimate is to obtain a price for each item you think you will need to purchase, from storm windows to paint, and add a per-hour fee for labor and profit. You may be able to do this yourself even before you discuss the specifics of the project with an architect or contractor, although you will need some knowledge of labor charges for various trades. Also, if you have specialized work to be done, such as repairing decorative plaster or woodwork, reproducing a beveled-glass door or special finishes, specific estimates will be needed.

Another way, and one that many people rely upon, is to ask relatives, friends and anyone else who is satisfied with a recently completed project what the various aspects of it cost. Go to their contractors and discuss the project. Always talk to more than one contractor or craftsperson, if possible.

If you have no previous experience with cost estimating or working with a contractor or craftsperson, then you may feel more comfortable hiring someone to do your estimating and negotiating for you. There is nothing wrong with this approach, and you might save a considerable amount of money. Architects, some historic preservation consultants and a few contractors will do this for a fee.

FUNDING TECHNIQUES

Here is a series of 14 steps you can follow to help fund a rehabilitation project. Several or all of these may work for you.

■ Obtain reliable advice on funding sources and economic benefits before you acquire an old house. Do not rely on hearsay. Check again periodically, as these financial sources and benefits can change quickly. If you are interested in donating an easement to a local nonprofit organization, you must realize that doing so takes planning and usually requires some professional assistance with the current federal tax laws.

■ Divide the project into manageable phases and be patient. Here is where careful planning can pay off. The most critical items, such as roofing, structural, electrical and mechanical work, should be done first so the house is livable. Beyond that, base your decisions on your needs, your budget and the availability of contractors and craftspersons.

■ Shop around for a lender. Rates are not the same everywhere, and you may be surprised by the difference one-quarter or one-half percent can make in the cost of a project.

■ Get a rehabilitation loan along with your original mortgage loan. Currently, funding the project in this manner has tax advantages, because the interest paid is a federal income tax deduction.

Rehabilitation project in a historic low- and moderate-income residential neighborhood in Savannah, Ga., which involved numerous public and private financial partners.

■ Investigate the possibility of borrowing against the equity in your home if you need money for a specific project after you have owned the house for awhile. Currently, the interest you pay on a home-equity loan can be deducted from your taxable income, just as the interest on your mortgage can.

■ If you find that the necessary repairs are more than you can afford, acquire a partner or partners to help you fund the work. (This is, in essence, what you are doing when you approach a lender). If you find yourself in a difficult financial situation, do not hesitate to scale the project down, carefully, to one that you can afford, or sell the house to someone who has the funds to undertake the work. Do not get in over your head and be forced later to make decisions that will be detrimental to the preservation of the house or to your sanity. Always have a written partnership agreement prepared by a professional. This agreement should spell out the procedure for buying out the portion of the project owned by your partners.

- Buy a double house so that you will have a source of income when you are finished. This tactic may also help you qualify for a mortgage and rehabilitation loan.

- Check at the local and state levels for grant and loan programs for which you may qualify. You may be eligible to lease or purchase a house that has been rehabilitated under a historic preservation revolving fund by a nonprofit group. Revolving funds, administered by a local or statewide nonprofit organization, are begun with a seed grant from a private or public source and are used for the acquisition and rehabilitation of historic properties that may or may not be clustered in one historic area. Following rehabilitation, the properties are sold or rented, with the proceeds going back to the fund, so it is continuously "revolving" and growing. Your house may be located in an area targeted for grants or low-interest rehabilitation loans administered by your local housing or community development office. Some cities conduct lotteries, offering "handyman specials" for a dollar. If you are a nonprofit organization, you may qualify for a number of funding programs.

- If your house has unusual or unique features, look for funding assistance or free labor from an organization that is especially interested in such examples of skilled work.

- Be creative in your approach to funding. Perhaps you are in a position to offer assistance to someone in exchange for labor or materials for your rehabilitation project.

- Offer your house as a training project, if appropriate, or as a model for the neighborhood. In this way you may qualify for assistance from a local organization or individual such as a trade school, neighborhood association or contractor.

- Save a certain sum of money each week for a specific project. Let your family know that you would like assistance with your rehabilitation project, so birthday and holiday gifts can be geared toward that goal.

- Rent the house, or part of it, for six months, a year or longer to someone else while you plan your rehabilitation

Above and right: On site
with a job-training program
in Michigan. Results were
dramatic. (Howard Page)

project and obtain the funds for it. You'll learn much more about the house and its needs, and you'll be glad you waited.

■ If your house is eligible for listing in the National Register of Historic Places, consider qualifying and applying for the federal rehabilitation tax credit and renting the house for five years (the minimum number of years currently required to avoid a penalty) before occupying it yourself. More information on the federal tax benefits is given in the next section.

Left: Sensitively executed rental residential rehabilitation project. The asphalt tile roof had been installed by a previous owner. The project was economically feasible because it qualified for a federal rehabilitation tax credit.

Below: In the same historic neighborhood, other owners have rehabilitated the carriage house at the rear of their property to serve as two apartments, thereby providing a source of income, along with a tax credit.

F ew programs or agencies extend grants and loans for preservation to individual homeowners and renters, except, of course, traditional loans from a bank. In general, unless you are rehabilitating housing for low-income persons or you represent a nonprofit organization such as a historical society or charitable group, you likely are not eligible for most public funding programs, or even for grants from private organizations, such as the National Trust for Historic Preservation. Also, very few grants are awarded for actual construction work. Most of the limited money available assists in hiring consultants to perform feasibility studies, analyses and other work necessary before actual repair is begun.

A tax credit for rehabilitation is available if the dwelling meets certain preservation standards and is income producing; owner-occupied dwelling units do not qualify. Some types of projects that might qualify are a home in which business is conducted, such as a bed-and-breakfast, or a rental apartment established in part of the house.

Below are some sources of funding to investigate if you feel that your organization or particular housing project would qualify. Addresses can be found under Information Sources in the back.

PUBLIC

Public funding sources for historic preservation include the U.S. Department of the Interior's Historic Preservation Fund, which grants matching monies to the state historic preservation offices for nonconstruction work, including surveys, the preparation of nominations to the National Register of Historic Places and historic preservation planning efforts. Following a six-year hiatus, the matching grants program for acquisition and development (construction) work for National Register–listed properties is active again but on a very limited basis. A portion of each state's federal allocation must go to those governments designated by the National Park Service as certified local governments, or CLGs. Priorities are determined

C. C. Thompson House, East Liverpool, Ohio. The owner, Columbiana County Historical Society, received a Historic Preservation Fund matching grant from the U.S. Department of the Interior through the state historic preservation office for basic roof repair and rehabilitation work. (Michael McCray)

jointly by the local government and the state office.

As mentioned above, the U.S. Department of the Treasury, in cooperation with the Department of the Interior and the state historic preservation offices, offers a 20 percent investment tax credit on the costs incurred in rehabilitating income-producing historic structures that meet certain criteria. The rehabilitation must qualify as "substantial" under federal rules, and all work must be certified by the U.S. Department of the Interior as meeting the Secretary of the Interior's Standards for Rehabilitation. Applications are available from, and must first be submitted to, the appropriate state historic preservation office. A federal tax deduction of the value of a conservation (historic preservation) easement granted in perpetuity to a qualified nonprofit organization or unit of government is also available. This is considered a charitable contribution. (For additional information on easements, see page 71.)

The U.S. Department of Housing and Urban Development (HUD) offers grants and loans for low- and moderate-income housing rehabilitation projects through its Community Development Block Grants and other programs, and individuals may qualify for these funds. HUD monies usually are administered locally by the county, village or city housing development office or authority. In cities, the funds often are directed toward certain targeted neighborhoods. Contact your local housing office for information.

The Federal National Mortgage Association (FNMA), or Fannie Mae, offers guaranteed loans for rehabilitation work based on the projected value of the property after rehabilitation. This program is administered locally through FNMA-approved lending institutions, and individuals qualify for the funds. Contact your local mortgage lender for information.

A growing number of states have historic preservation grant and loan programs, and some have state income tax credits. Also, state arts and humanities agencies or councils may offer grants for nonconstruction historic preservation projects such as exhibits, surveys, workshops and publications.

County or community historic preservation grant and loan programs are available in some localities. Check with your local or state historic preservation office for information. Assistance could include abatement of property taxes or funds from local arts or humanities agencies.

PRIVATE

The National Trust for Historic Preservation administers several financial assistance programs in conjunction with its seven regional and field offices. All grant and loan programs apply to urban and rural areas and are available only to nonprofit organizations that are National Trust Preservation Forum members. National Trust programs include low-interest loans, loan guaranties and lines of credit, through the National Preservation Loan Fund, to assist nonprofit organizations or public agencies in creating or expanding preservation revolving funds or initiating real estate development projects to preserve historic buildings, sites and districts. A special endangered properties component of the program provides loans for threatened National Historic Landmarks. For this part of the program, the applicant need not be a nonprofit organization or public agency. Matching grants to nonprofit groups and public agencies are available through the Preservation Services Fund to initiate preservation projects such as feasibility studies. Grants, low-interest loans and technical assistance are made possible through the Inner-City Ventures Fund to nonprofit neighborhood associations for rehabilitation projects aimed at revitalizing historic neighborhoods for the benefit of low- and moderate-income residents, especially minorities.

In addition to the National Trust, some national and state-based private endowments, foundations and funds may provide resources for both nonconstruction and construction projects, particularly those of national significance. These sources can vary considerably, depending on the project. If, for example, you need funds for the rehabilitation of a house that figured prominently in the Civil War, then check the *Foundation Directory* (see page 197) for philanthropic organizations specifically interested in this era and type of project. Remember that any funds would likely be available only to nonprofit organizations, not to individuals.

On the state and regional levels, some private historic preservation organizations have grant and loan programs or preservation revolving funds. Check with your statewide private historic preservation organization or state historic preservation office for information on programs in your area.

In addition to national and state programs, a number of local historic preservation organizations and historical societies provide grants and loans for preservation projects. Local preservation revolving funds are generally community-wide or restricted to work in certain historic neighborhoods. Check with your local or state historic preservation office for more information on the availability of these resources.

If you feel you may qualify, do not overlook the possibility of obtaining a grant from a local private endowment, foundation, philanthropic organization or individual. Many nonprofit organizations preserving a historic house have found that local businesses are interested in becoming associated with their project by making a donation of products or services, not only for the rehabilitation or restoration of the house, but also for events held there. Donations of design and printing services, food, flowers and furnishings are common.

TEN MONEY-SAVING TIPS

All of us are interested in the most economical approach to fixing up, dressing up and just plain repairing our homes. Here are some ideas that will, in particular, help you to rehabilitate respectfully and wisely.

1. Purchase the right house. Remember that a minimalist approach is always a money-saving one. Plan to purchase a house that requires the fewest changes to meet your needs. Why buy a house that will need a large addition to accommodate your family when another house that already has enough space is available nearby? You will be doing the building — and yourself — a favor if you choose a house that closely matches your needs and tastes as it is. Don't try to remake a building into something it isn't — you'll be spending a lot of money, you may not be pleased with the results and you may very well have destroyed much of the building's historic fabric along the way. Also, selling a house that has been highly customized is very difficult. It will appeal only to a handful of potential buyers, and others will be thinking about what it will cost them to undo what you have done.

2. Plan carefully and deliberately. You are asking for trouble and unnecessary expenses if you make quick decisions and barge ahead with rehabilitation work. By living with the house before making major rehabilitation plans, you can save money. When you first examine the old windows, for example, they may appear to be too deteriorated to save, but if you inspect them carefully and individually, you may discover that, while some parts may need to be replaced, all in all they are in relatively good condition and can be rehabilitated.

3. Seek expert advice. Check with experts before purchasing a product or service with which you are unfamiliar.

Left and below: Misinformed effort to save money and make old houses "maintenance free." Owners of these two properties have boarded up windows in preparation for vinyl or aluminum siding, even over masonry. In addition, historic porches and other features have been removed and replaced with modern substitutes that are visually unsuited to the historic buildings, thus destroying the character of the houses and undermining the character of the entire historic neighborhood. Note also that an unaltered house is being demolished.

You may find that the item or the procedure is unnecessary, overpriced or even counterproductive. You can save both money and effort by not doing that work.

4. Be patient and maintain an open mind. You may discover another approach, perhaps in a neighbor's house or a magazine article, that will accomplish what you want but cost significantly less and, even better, involve fewer changes to the historic house.

5. Establish priorities. After you have completed your project planning, assign priority to all the work you want to do and do it in that order. This approach will save you money in the long run. Interior work could be done during the colder months, the off-season when contractors may give you a better price. Some work, such as plumbing, heating, cooling and electrical work, should be done early. If there is any question about the viability of the plumbing system, for example, have it inspected thoroughly before repairing and repainting the ornate plaster ceiling below it!

6. Know your rehabilitation strategy. Have a fairly specific idea of what you want to do before talking to someone you may hire to do it. This advice holds true for anyone you may hire, from architects to storm window installers. Most contractors are not designers. They will build the interior partition where you say you want it. You will waste their time and your money if you change your mind about its placement after the work has started. Also, a consultant, contractor or craftsperson, sensing that you may not be sure of what you want, will be more likely to charge you by the hour or may demand a higher-than-usual flat fee.

7. Get references. Do not expect superior work from an inexperienced consultant, contractor or craftsperson, and do not expect to pay bargain-basement rates for experts. Those who have had to pay to have work redone — and this is more common than you may think — will tell you that a bargain can be very expensive in the end.

8. Do some work yourself. Consider doing some of the labor yourself if you have the time, the desire and some basic skills. Very few residential rehabilitation projects are accomplished without some sweat equity, and it can be a real money saver. Many people have found that removing wallpaper or repainting woodwork is a great way to relax after a day at the office. Also, you can easily and immediately see the progress you have made, which can be very rewarding.

9. Have related work done together. Attempt to have all related work done at one time or at least sign a single, multiphased contract with each person or company. Piecemeal contracts can be much more expensive. Try to avoid having any leftover work; a return trip will cost more than extra time on the original job. If you are hiring a cabinetmaker to build shelves in a closet, for example, combine that project with any other work for which you need a cabinetmaker, such as kitchen cabinets or woodwork repair.

10. Watch the thermostat. Avoid heating or cooling the house to human comfort levels if it is unoccupied during construction work. If workers are in and out of the house all day, it may be wise to turn the heating or cooling system down or off. When the house is occupied, keep the thermostat low in the winter months, high during the summer, and wear a heavy sweater in the winter and very lightweight clothing in the summer.

Window maintenance. A tried-and-true way to save money is to do the labor-intensive work yourself. Here a volunteer is repainting window frames during the restoration of a Gothic Revival school in Marshall, Mich. (NTHP)

BEFORE YOU BEGIN

Because rehabilitation is by far the most common approach used in the physical preservation of a historic house, very likely describing more than 90 percent of all projects undertaken, this term is used throughout the next three chapters, which deal with maintenance, repair and construction. An overall rehabilitation effort may include different treatments for specific problems, such as repairing a stairway balustrade, restoring a cornice and box gutter damaged by wind and water and reconstructing a missing porch or mantelpiece. The term rehabilitation as used here encompasses all these tasks that together form the typical old-house project.

Above: Dormers and a cobblestone chimney on a Gothic Revival residence. Some particularly ornate, vulnerable features such as these will need special attention in any rehabilitation or maintenance plans.

FINDING AND BUYING AN OLD HOUSE

As real estate professionals have said for years, the three factors most important in buying and selling real estate are location, location and location. This is as true for historic houses as it is for new houses. The urban pioneers who purchased homes in deteriorating neighborhoods in the 1960s and 1970s often paid very little for their houses, but they were taking a risk — as it turned out, often a worthwhile risk. Purchasing a residence in many of these same neighborhoods today requires an investment of several hundred thousand dollars. In some cities it is still possible to purchase a condemned house for one dollar, agree to bring it up to code within a certain number of months and occupy it for a specified number of years, but you will be taking a risk similar to that assumed by the urban homesteaders of 25 years ago. Whether this approach is for you is a decision only you can make.

Opposite: Modest Queen Anne house in Silverton, Colo., probably before 1940. During the 1940s, the house was covered with asbestos siding, the gingerbread removed and the porch enclosed. Since then the house has been restored to some of its former glory. (Russell Lee)

Modest houses along a shaded street in Collinsville, Conn., where trees contribute to the neighborhood's intimacy. (Ted Ancher)

Home-buying assistance is easy to find. Schools, real estate professionals and financial institutions commonly offer basic seminars and written materials. However, in most areas of the country few, if any, agents or organizations can provide accurate data on finding a suitable historic house to accommodate your needs. Therefore, in addition to seeking out the basic real estate courses, you may wish to check with community or neighborhood associations, historical societies or historic preservation organizations for assistance.

Develop a list of what you want in a historic house deliberately and carefully. Many old-house buyers say that they began simply by inspecting houses for sale in the general locations they preferred, looking at what was available and affordable, and developing a list of must-haves and don't-wants as they went along. Of course, the house you end up with may have some features you do not want, but be wary of falling in love with fancy woodwork or a romantic alcove, ignoring the fact that the building has only two bedrooms and you need four.

If you find that very few or none of the old houses that you have seen appeal to you or seem to have what you want or if you like the exteriors of old houses but cannot imagine living in one without first making major changes to the way the rooms relate to one another, then perhaps old-house living is not for you. If you have always lived in a new house or apartment, you may want to rent an old house for a while before purchasing a place of your own. Remember that an old house will never be perfect, which of course is part of its charm. The uneven plaster, the pesky creak in the dining room floor and the door that never closes just right are all part of the unique character of an old house.

Your list of priorities can be somewhat flexible, of course, but it should include everything. Refer to the accompanying sample list prepared for an imaginary family of four. Typical concerns are the number and uses of rooms and their arrangement, along with room sizes, which may or may not be very important to you. The presence of an attic and a basement, finished or not, may also be a consideration. Amenities such as whole-house cooling, a swimming pool, a patio or deck or a well-landscaped yard may be essential. On the other hand, you may not want any of these features, particularly the ones that can represent a lot of maintenance work. If a large lawn, for example, does not appeal to you, you should obviously not be looking for a house in a neighborhood where large lawns are a major design feature.

This advice seems so simple, but potential buyers often do not grasp the realities of living in the neighborhood to which they are attracted until they purchase a house and move in. Take some time to talk to the people you see in the area about the specifics of day-to-day living. Is this residential area densely populated, affording little privacy? Is it a noisy neighborhood, perhaps because of its proximity to a major industry? Is it a neighborhood where people drive their automobiles and rarely walk anywhere? Is it a tourist destination? (To many potential buyers these traits are not disadvantages. Many individuals and families seek out neighborhoods with one or more of these features.) You naturally will obtain information about schools, churches or synagogues, parks and other recreational facilities, and transportation systems as part of your investigation into the neighborhood.

Investigate unconventional sources in your quest for a suitable historic house. Your old-house hunting efforts should go beyond a search through the real estate advertisements in the Sunday newspaper. Let a number of people who are associated in some way with local history know that you are searching for a particular type of house in a particular location. Local library personnel can generally steer you to these people if you need help in finding them. Visit the neighborhood frequently, looking for for-sale or for-rent signs. When you see people outside working on their houses or in their gardens, tell them that you are looking for a house to purchase or lease. They may know of a house that will come on the market in a few weeks or months.

Similarly, check with real estate agents who work in the area. They usually know of houses not yet on the market but possibly available soon. Give as accurate a description as possible of what you want. Be aware that most real estate professionals do not know architectural history, so make it clear that when you say you are looking for a Greek Revival–style house or a bungalow you mean an authentic historic house, not one built recently that may be similar in appearance to these. Also, be certain that they know the general appearance of the sort of house you are seeking; the agent may know that style or type of house by another name. You might want to provide photographs of houses similar to what you are looking for or drive through the neighborhood, pointing out examples of houses you like. Most real estate professionals will welcome the opportunity to work with you and will be very helpful. You may, in fact, find that you have a number of excellent houses to choose from, each meeting your basic requirements.

You may want to try a bold approach if you see a particular house that you like very much. Simply knock on the door and ask if it is for sale. It may be! Of course, the interior may be a disappointment to you, and the price may not be close to what you were prepared to pay. But at least you will have learned something.

Speaking of price, finding a historic house priced far below what it is truly worth is rare today, but real bargains can be found, particularly if you are in no hurry to purchase. The price will be considerably lower in some smaller communities that are at least 45 minutes by automobile or train from a much larger urban area. It is estimated that you can save 20 to 40 percent on the cost of almost any house by purchasing in one of these communities or by purchasing rural property.

An inspection of the property you intend to buy is a must. Many buyers have an independent house inspection done by a professional consultant before purchasing property. In such cases, an inspection is a contingency in the purchase contract. If major problems are revealed during the inspection, the contract may be renegotiated or voided. You may also conduct one yourself. If you discover a problem, then you will want to hire a professional to investigate and advise you.

HOW TO INSPECT A HOUSE

An old house should be thoroughly and formally inspected, top to bottom, at least once a year, but not at the same time each year. One goal of inspection is to find out how the various parts and systems of the house function during different seasons and weather conditions, including a range of temperatures and high and low relative humidity. In fact, an excellent time to inspect the house is during a rainstorm; you will be able to ascertain where the water is going after it hits the roof! Also, if you can, carefully observe the house for several days after a snowstorm to see if, and how, the snow melts and where the water goes. These observations can tell you if heat is escaping through the roof or if water is being shed properly, and they provide essential clues as to why certain repairs are needed and why previous owners replaced, or removed, features.

Any information you have already gathered about the physical condition of the house will be of use. You may have conducted a study of the house while completing a historic inventory form for it, for example, or you may have done some investigating to determine when and in what order various sections of the house were constructed or how it was altered over the years. All this physical research, along with written and oral sources, will assist you in your in-depth inspection.

Ornate cast-iron fence in New Orleans. Features such as this should be part of a thorough site inspection. (Carleton Knight III)

First, prepare a file that includes the following:

- List of items from previous inspections to recheck, if any
- Results of research on the building's physical history, including information on additions and other known changes
- Sketches of the floor plans, the roof plan and outline elevations, also essential in locating problem areas for future reference

Review all this information before starting your inspection.

EXTERIOR INSPECTION

Start at the roof and work downward. If your roof is steeply pitched or is difficult to reach, use binoculars to search for potential problem areas. Depending on what you find, you may want to have a professional roofer or other consultant look closely at the roof later. Look particularly

Pages from Gustav Stickley's *Craftsman Homes*, 1909. Books about exterior and interior residential design exist for virtually every period of American architectural history. Stickley's book is very useful in researching the original floor plans and appearance, both inside and out, of examples of an important phase of early 20th-century house design. (Peregrine Smith Books)

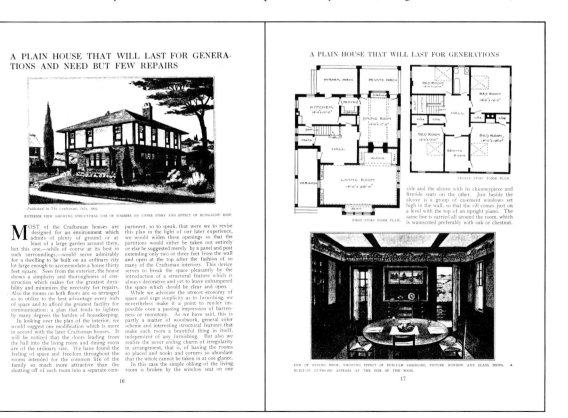

at the chimneys, ventilators, vent pipes, parapets, copings, ridges, valleys, and the roofing and flashing around each of these. Check for missing mortar in the chimneys. Note gaps or missing roofing or flashing, low spots where water has collected, areas where tree branches have hit the roof and the presence of mold or moss. Record the location of problem areas on the roof plan drawing.

Investigate every section of the eaves, gutters and downspouts. Look particularly for missing pieces, poor connections, undersized gutters and downspouts (these will be evident during a hard rainstorm), and confirm that water is being carried away from the foundation and not draining into or next to it. Look for areas of ice or snow buildup in the winter, including the presence of icicles.

Next inspect the exterior walls for stains, vines and their residue, moss and mildew, damaged masonry or siding, larger-than-normal gaps in the siding, cracks in the masonry, missing mortar, paint failure and insect damage. Look along each wall to check for bulges or areas that are out of plumb. Mark the specific location of problem areas on the elevation sketches. Note the presence of round plugs, an indication that the house has blown-in insulation. For a house with more than one layer of siding, you may want to remove portions of the cover-up material in inconspicuous locations to reveal the original wood.

Check the foundation next, paying special attention to missing or loose sections, cracks and shifts in the masonry, roots, shrubs, trees, vines and other plants at or near the walls. Does the foundation appear to be wet as the result of rising damp? Ground water rises in masonry by capillary action, and evidence of a wet site may show up on the exterior at the foundation and walls. Look for seismic anchors, if the house is located in an area of the country that requires or encourages their installation. Take another look at the points at which the downspouts meet the ground or the eaves drain onto the ground. Is water being carried away from the foundation and basement of the house?

Inspect the entire site carefully, looking for low spots where water may collect and other signs of poor water drainage. Note the location of any old wells or cisterns. These may be leaking into the basement.

Look at each window and door, at the same time checking the walls again for evidence of deterioration or

Above: House inspection starts with the roof. This wood-shingle roof appears to be in excellent condition, but a closer inspection from a ladder, from the second floor windows—to inspect the porch roof—and from the dormer windows is necessary.

Left: Deterioration revealed during a periodic inspection. Potentially damaging plants protrude between the concrete walk and the stone foundation, and new mortar from a poor stone repointing job has fallen out.

Oriel window with leaded-glass casement sash, a significant feature of this house's facade. Paint failure indicates a moisture problem, possibly due in part to the plant growth on the walls.

water problems. Look at each hoodmold, arch, lintel, jamb, sill and sash, checking for deteriorated masonry, wood or metal, broken glass, failed caulking, poor weatherstripping and chipped paint. Also note the presence and condition of storm sash. Record your findings on the elevation sketches.

Complete your exterior investigation by taking a good look at the porches, bay windows and other exterior features that project from the exterior walls or are recessed into them. Note any deterioration you observe.

Start your interior inspection in the attic. Here you may be very glad you wore an old shirt! Be on the lookout for areas that are or have been wet. Note whether the ventilation is adequate. Be sure to bring with you the notes you took during the exterior roof inspection. You will want to get an interior view of any exterior roof problems, and you should not rely on memory alone in locating these. Check the condition of the wood rafters and other structural members by inserting your pocket knife into the wood at an angle and then lifting it up sharply. Sound wood will separate in long, thin splinters; deteriorated wood will either disintegrate or come away in short, broken splinters. Note the location, type and thickness of any insulation and whether or not it has a vapor barrier.

Check each room or area of the interior carefully for any

Inaccessible attic area. Attic inspection must include all parts. Here boards, not visible, placed over the joists provide safe footing for a close look.

Above: Using the knife test to check the soundness of floor joists.

Right: Old termite damage. Although the first floor joists had appeared sound, probing with a knife revealed this basement damage.

water damage, looking first at ceilings and the exterior walls for damaged or loose plaster (you may need to poke at it in a number of places), peeling wallpaper or paint failure. Note any floors that are obviously not level. Look particularly for leaks around and under windows and fireplaces. Check each area where you noted an exterior problem. Mark on the floor plans any problems you observe.

Open and close each window and door, checking for ease of operation, broken sash cords and faulty hardware.

Examine features such as mantelpieces and stairways carefully, determining both the overall and piece-by-piece condition, using your knife again, if necessary, to check for soundness of wood. Examine metal elements such as door and window hardware and mantels, and note needed repairs.

Next, spend lots of time in the basement or crawl space checking, both visually and with the knife test, the soundness of the wood structural members. Is there evidence of dry rot, termites, carpenter ants or other insects and, therefore, unsound wood? Again, carefully record the locations of problems to assist a consultant or contractor. Is there evidence of past or present structural problems? Have extra supports been added? Note the location, type and thickness of any insulation. Does it have a vapor barrier? Pay particular attention to the presence of moisture on the walls or floors. Is there standing water? Is the humidity high? Is the ventilation adequate?

Check the type of water supply pipes. Copper pipes generally indicate that the plumbing has been replaced and updated. Look for signs of old or current leaks. Note the location of all vertical runs — where pipes run vertically from floor to floor. If these are near the outside walls and you live in an area with harsh winters, you may want to relocate these lines when you have them replaced. Natural gas pipes should be tested by a professional; do-it-yourself tests often are unreliable.

Inspect the heating, cooling and ventilating systems for indications that they have been serviced regularly or at least recently. If they have not, have them inspected by a professional. Check the temperature in each room by using a thermometer, and note any problems with individual heating, cooling or ventilating units, radiators or registers.

Determine the type of electrical service and wiring the

house has. Count the number of wires going into the service box on the outside of the house. Three-wire service of at least 150 amperes is necessary for the safe and efficient operation of a house with an electric range, clothes dryer and central air conditioning. Most old houses whose wiring has not been updated in the last 25 years or so will not have this type of service. If the wiring is inadequate or outdated, do not assume that the entire house will need to be rewired. Note the number of outlets in each room or area of the house and determine if they are adequate for your needs. At this point, you may want to go to an electrical contractor for advice about the level of electrical service you need for your lifestyle.

Finally, return to any areas to make further investigation, if needed, or to check conflicting data. Take notes and make observations while you are still looking at the parts of the house, if possible. Don't rely on memory. Keep all your notes, sketches and photographs available for quick reference.

Conduct another inspection, perhaps just of problem areas, at an appropriate time — for instance, after the leaves fall, so that you can check the condition of the gutters, or during the coldest time of the year, so that you can determine whether you need to install ventilation fans in the rooms with the highest humidity.

ESSENTIAL MAINTENANCE

Very simply, maintenance is the continuing care and repair of both the interior and the exterior of your historic house. It means that cleaning is done on a regular basis, that casual inspections, in addition to the formal inspections discussed above, are conducted according to a schedule and that repairs are anticipated and completed without delay. It also means that emergency work is done immediately and well. If a temporary solution to a problem is necessary, then the permanent remedy is planned and undertaken as soon as possible. In this manner, the inevitable temporary fix-up does not lead to a costly, long-term repair. Most important, good maintenance assumes a great deal of diligence, resulting in few, if any, major repairs.

CASUAL INSPECTIONS

Don't overlook the opportunity to check the condition of your house. Inspect the interior and exterior of your house including the site on a regular basis, at different times of the year and during different weather conditions. Look particularly carefully at the parts of the house most exposed to the weather. Each time you drive by is a good time to observe the roof and chimneys; damage from wind or other cause can occur at any time.

Get into the habit of casually checking out the exterior

Sign of loving care. As shown by this well-cared-for picturesque historic house, continuous inspection and minor work are part of good maintenance and essential to avoid expensive major repairs and rebuilding. (Ohio Historic Preservation Office)

Above: Restored wood-shingle roof. Roofs, even those newly restored to their original material and appearance, need constant inspection and damage assessment.

Right: Edge of shingle roof, gutter and downspout. Close observation of gutters is essential to determine their condition. Large trees surrounding this roof make bimonthly inspection necessary.

of the house every time you walk around it. You may, for example, find you need to pull up vines every month.

On the interior, while performing your regular cleaning tasks, go over conditions in each room or area of the house on a rotating basis, looking for broken panes of glass, tell-tale cracks and other signs of moisture penetration, wear and tear or damage. The idea is to correct little problems, such as water leaks, before they turn into big problems, such as a room of ruined plaster. You can never ignore maintenance tasks. If you do, your negligence will return to haunt you, costing you more in the long run.

Everyday Maintenance

Train family members in proper techniques for watering houseplants, mopping up spills, opening and closing windows and doors and other normal activities that involve the historic features of the house. Teach everyone to respect these historic materials and features.

Wash windows frequently. This simple procedure can actually result in energy savings by allowing light and heat in.

Purchase and use equipment and products appropriate and recommended for the tasks you are performing. An industrial window cleaning solution, for example, may clean your windows well but may also damage paint or varnish. In fact, many industrial products may be too harsh for any home setting.

Periodic Maintenance

Plan maintenance tasks. For you and your house this strategy may be a time set aside each week or month to do work that needs to be done, or it may be establishing a contractual agreement with a roofer who will inspect and repair any damaged areas on a regular basis, perhaps every six months or so.

Do not make changes in the historic features of your house simply for maintenance reasons, for instance, painting woodwork or walls a dark color so dirt will not show, installing aluminum or vinyl siding or removing hard-to-reach trim. Some old houses are undoubtedly more difficult

Right: Potentially harmful ivy. Vining plants grow surprisingly quickly and can take over a wall in less than a month. Here it is best to cut the vines at ground level, let them dry out, then pull them off the building. Remember, however, they still will grow back.

Below: Covered basement window. Basement windows should be opened when the weather warms in the spring. In this case, a screen in the opening would serve the purpose well. Year-round light and ventilation to basement and attic spaces, however, are recommended.

to maintain than new ones, but this fact should be recognized before purchasing an old house. Nothing can be expected to be maintenance-free.

Use equipment and products according to the manufacturer's directions and be sure that you are properly trained. Following this simple advice could spare you illness and serious injury. For example, do not stand on the top rung of a stepladder. Likewise, if a facial mask should be worn while using a certain toxic product, then purchase and use the mask.

On a regular basis, check and clean or replace filters that are part of your heating, cooling and ventilating systems.

Repair immediately any plumbing problems such as a dripping faucet or clogged drain.

Consider hiring someone to do routine maintenance work and cleaning such as removing leaves from gutters, caulking windows and patching plaster rather than waiting until a problem develops. You will likely save money in the long run if you have someone do the ongoing maintenance work for you. If you cannot afford this service, handle these routine tasks yourself.

Below left: Fallen-away downspout. The force of rainwater has removed mortar between the bricks, causing moisture to penetrate the interior where plaster damage has already occurred.

**Below right: Poor caulking between a window jamb and brick wall. The caulking must be removed and replaced, otherwise water will damage the wood and eventually find its way into the house.
The paint is being allowed to peel away from the historically unpainted sandstone window sill.**

HOW TO GET THE WORK DONE

WITHOUT GOING INSANE

Whether you are doing some of the work yourself or are hiring others to do all of it, working on an old house presents problems and conflicts that can be both upsetting and unsettling in an owner's daily life. If you are uneasy or unsure about the direction of any work, get a second, or third, opinion. This will allow you to sit back and take a more objective look before moving on.

Do not rush to start the work immediately. If possible, live in the house first before finalizing your major rehabilitation decisions and before setting priorities for doing the work. At the very least, spend time in the house removing trash and cleaning everything well. Wait until after the cleanup is finished before making decisions.

You can buy some time by completing your literary and oral history study and physical inspection of the house before doing anything else. Then, identify the house's character-defining features and plan the appropriate and necessary type of work for each — maintenance, repair, restoration and so on. In addition, prepare lists of all other necessary work and put these steps in order; organize by type (electrical, for example), location or both.

Get a realistic idea of what you are facing by talking to other homeowners, preferably in your neighborhood or community, who have completed projects similar to yours. From them you will find out how long a project actually takes, what to watch out for and, most important, what they would do differently.

Before commencing work, familiarize yourself with and obtain all building permits and other approvals. If you are in a locally designated historic district, for example, you will need to obtain a certificate of appropriateness for any work to the house, particularly any work that changes even slightly the exterior appearance. Perhaps the house is located in a state historic district that has similar requirements. Find out how much time the various approvals are likely to take and build this additional time into your project timetable.

Sanded paint on a wood porch post. The owner's research revealed that sanded paint, a specialized painting technique meant to simulate stone, was used on this Italianate house.

Resist the temptation to do major work that is irreversible. You may be very surprised at what you discover. For example, the room that you initially thought would be an ideal master bedroom may prove to have drawbacks that were not apparent at first. Some planning and a trial period could have indicated another room as a better choice. Many of the houses advertised in the local newspaper as handyman specials likely got in that condition not because of neglect but because the owners gutted them immediately after purchasing and then ran out of money and enthusiasm for the project.

When you do begin actual construction, complete the basic structural, exterior, window, mechanical and electrical work for the whole house first, starting at the foundation and working up. If there is a section of the building you will not be rehabilitating immediately, be certain to protect and stabilize it early in the project.

On the interior, finish one entire room first. Reaching an intermediate goal like this will boost your confidence and give you a place to which to retreat. Also, it lets you know quite accurately how long the entire project will take, how much it will cost and possibly what you can and cannot do yourself. Many people have found that the best way to avoid panic is to finish the project room by room, particularly if they are doing a sizable part of the rehabilitation work themselves.

Try your best to be flexible and realistic, even if your goal is to finish the work in time for holiday entertaining, returning to teaching in the fall or any other deadline you have set. Remember that construction work is affected by weather, the labor market and delivery schedules. On the other hand, do not be so lenient that those who are doing the work may be tempted to take advantage of you.

Rejoice in the purchase of your historic home and the progress you are making with its rehabilitation by having an informal "before" open house, an in-progress get-together and, naturally, an "after" party. Make an occasion of an event like the completion of the kitchen or the exterior or woodwork refinishing by going on a short trip or having an at-home vacation of a few days.

Do not be afraid to terminate a relationship with a consultant, architect or contractor with whom you have problems after first discussing the situation openly and attempting to come to a mutual understanding. After all, the problem could be a simple misunderstanding on your part. Inevitably, some disputes end up in the courts, but this should be a last resort. All contracts should be professionally prepared and reviewed by an attorney to be sure that you are protected.

Rethink your goals and timetable if you have unexpected financial or personal problems or if you find yourself losing interest in the project. After many weeks, months and even years of effort, it is very difficult, if not impossible, to remain as enthusiastic as you were at the start of a project.

This letdown happens to everybody. Perhaps the best — or only — solution is to stop work for a period of time, seek professional advice or acquire a partner. Assuming you have done your advance planning well, you could, as a last resort, sell the house to someone who is willing to pay for the work that you have already completed.

HIRING AND WORKING WITH PROFESSIONALS

The task of locating excellent professional help for planning and executing an old-house rehabilitation project is often a difficult one. Unfortunately, it is sometimes made more difficult as a result of poor planning. For example, although you may not know whether you will want or need to hire an engineer, architect or landscape architect when you start looking for a house to purchase, you will certainly want to consider the potential cost in any preliminary rehabilitation budget. The same holds true for hiring a preservation consultant, such as an archeologist, historian or architectural historian.

Many people rely on friends and relatives for advice about qualified professionals. This approach may work well if the projects your friends and relatives have undertaken involve work to historic buildings and are similar to your project. A better idea might be to check with your neighborhood association, local historic preservation official or state historic preservation office for advice. Some of these organizations maintain lists of qualified and recommended archeologists, architects and other consultants, contractors and craftspersons. Also, most will be able to tell you about preservation procedures and products to avoid.

You may want to consider having a qualified consultant prepare what is often called a historic structure report for your house. It includes all the written, oral and physical information gathered while researching the history and physical development of the house. It also includes the results of the house inspection, with detailed information about the present condition of all the building's parts and systems as well as specific recommendations about what work needs to be done — and in what order — to rehabilitate

Right and opposite: Much-altered Greek Revival porch before and after restoration. In-depth research, together with professional advice, was essential for this project.

and maintain the house. Photographs and drawings also are usually integrated into the report. Depending on your own wishes and the approach followed by the consultant you hire, you may be able to do some of the work for the report yourself.

Try, if possible, to obtain proposals and cost estimates from at least two qualified contractors, and do not fail to check the references of anyone you are considering hiring, including persons who come highly recommended by

friends or family members. Thus, you must obtain a list of clients who have completed projects similar to yours. Talk to these clients and personally inspect the work done by the consultant, contractor or craftsperson.

After you have selected a person or company to hire, discuss the terms of the contract, which you both will sign. Get as much as possible in writing. The contract should cover the following items:

- Detailed descriptions of work and methods

- Permits
- Schedules
- Cleanup and debris removal
- Payment amounts and due dates
- Resolution of conflicts
- Changes or substitutions to the work
- Provision for subcontractors

Be sure that the contractor you hire is licensed to do the work. Bonding is also an important consideration. Check both your insurance coverage and your consultant's or contractor's coverage, as it is likely that your homeowner's policy will not cover persons who are being paid to perform work on your house.

If a problem arises, such as construction work that is not satisfactory to you, bring it to the attention of the consultant, architect or contractor immediately. Do not wait for the work to get better. The problem may be due to a simple misunderstanding or misinterpretation of the contract provisions.

BUILDING CODES AND OTHER REGULATIONS

Most major state building codes now contain sections or special provisions designed specifically to apply to work on old buildings constructed before a certain date. The provisions do not exempt these buildings from code compliance; rather, they allow for substitutions in cases where strict adherence to the general code would make rehabilitation economically infeasible or work would result in the destruction of architecturally and historically significant elements. In addition, some cities have their own code regulations that apply to old buildings or buildings in certain well-defined categories.

While some code provisions do not apply to single- or two-family residences, nearly any project involving work on a house will require a local building permit. In addition, work such as wiring, plumbing, heating, ventilating, air conditioning, roof replacement and any structural repairs may require special permits, inspections and licenses.

PRACTICAL ADVICE FOR DO-IT-YOURSELFERS

Do not plan to do all the work yourself, unless it is minimal or you are a professional contractor or craftsperson and have ample time to devote to the project. In some areas you must be licensed to do certain work, so check before you start any project. At the same time, obtain the necessary building permits and other approvals you will need. Do only the work you can do well, want to do and enjoy doing.

Remember that every task requires some knowledge and skill. Do not make the mistake of barging ahead with a project and then learning how to do it. If you have never done any painting, for example, do not assume that you just dip the brush into the paint and spread it on the surface in any manner. Painting, along with everything else, takes knowledge, skill and patience.

If you have the desire and the time, learn new skills by taking classes at trade schools or working with a skilled craftsperson. A number of books provide step-by-step instructions for doing almost everything connected with rehabilitating an old house. And you will become more proficient through experience.

Consider organizing an informal neighborhood cooperative to do work on each of the members' houses, sharing your skills with others. Perhaps, for example, you are experienced at plumbing but lack carpentry skills. An "exchange program" would benefit everyone.

Develop and follow a timetable that is both realistic and flexible, with built-in days off; have available and use the correct equipment, tools and supplies for each job you do.

Be careful. Remember that most accidents occur in the home. Even the simplest task can result in injury if you do not follow instructions. Do not take short cuts.

Hire someone else to do the remainder of the work if you find that the project is too much for you. Of course, no contractor or craftsperson likes to finish work begun by someone else, so you may want to complete a phase of the work yourself, just to provide a clean start for the new worker. However, if it has taken months to partly remove wallpaper from one room, no one will fault you for hiring someone else to finish. You'll be amazed at how quickly it goes with help!

OUTSIDE THE OLD HOUSE

The exterior of any building must be cared for to ensure the existence of the entire structure. This important exterior work, whether it is maintenance or actual rehabilitation, is often neglected in favor of cosmetic treatments that may look good, at least for a time, but do not contribute to the preservation of the building. This chapter offers a common-sense approach to exterior rehabilitation that is sensitive to a building's important characteristics. Included are general points to consider as well as specific advice with regard to parts of the exterior.

If you are planning to adapt your house, or part of it, to meet the requirements of a business or to create an apartment, be particularly careful. If major changes are necessary to adapt a property to a new use, such as site alterations or removing several windows, then perhaps the property is not suitable for the purposes intended. In any case, you should determine the character-defining features and strive to preserve these. If you are planning to take advantage of the federal rehabilitation tax credit, you most likely will need the advice of a professional before beginning work to ensure your project meets the minimum historic preservation requirements.

Above:Porch post with scrollwork ornamentation, also known as gingerbread. (T. Wrenn)

EXTERIOR MATERIALS AND FEATURES

Learning about the building materials that compose your dwelling and with which you are working will help you gain an understanding of how and why they deteriorate and how to repair them to avoid problems in the future. These materials may have very different characteristics from ones with which you may be more familiar.

Opposite: Painting the porch of a Victorian residence. Special care must be taken in the use of ladders. (Jack E. Boucher)

Wood and masonry are by far the most common building materials, both for houses and other buildings. Most likely a number of different woods have been used in your house. Masonry can include adobe, brick, stone, concrete, various types of formed block, and stucco. Architectural metals, both structural and decorative, include cast and wrought iron, steel, copper, bronze, nickel, aluminum and various galvanized and plated metals. Glass and plastics such as vinyl are used frequently today.

Your house will have special features that are important visually and are historically and architecturally significant. A series of brackets under a cornice may seem rather mundane, but remember that such features are significant to the overall composition. Sadly, many people discover how important these small features are only after they remove them and wonder what happened to the special character of the house. Prepare a list of the significant features of your house and do not tamper with the form and materials of these items in any rehabilitation projects you undertake. Special architectural features of primary importance to the appearance and function of historic houses include porches, entrances, balconies, dormers, bay and oriel windows, and towers and turrets. Even the simplest folk or traditional house has elements such as a water table or distinctive wood trim that give it character.

Here are a few points to consider before you begin to work with exterior materials:

■ Respect the unique characteristics of the various architectural materials with which you are dealing by using cleaning and other products designed specifically for that material.

■ Remember that some building materials were disguised historically, particularly during the second half of the 19th century. Do not assume, for example, that what looks like marble is actually marble (it might be painted wood) or that what looks like wood is wood (it might be pressed sheet metal).

■ Plan to use substitute materials only in cases where the original material clearly is not durable or where the cost or availability of the original material precludes its use. Not all building materials or design details used historically are durable or were good for the purpose intended. Sometimes these materials deteriorate and must be replaced or the

Above and left: Richardsonian Romanesque residence in Kearney, Neb. The character of the house changed dramatically with changes to the roof as well as the surrounding porch.

faulty design must be changed. Any unavoidable substitutions or alterations in materials or design should respect the form and details of the original feature.

- Consider using newer techniques, such as epoxy consolidation, to preserve deteriorated wood. This will save the

133

Problems Caused by Moisture

Most old-house deterioration is caused either directly or indirectly by the presence of water, either as a liquid or in vapor form. The following common exterior deterioration problems are caused by moisture:

Wet rot, the deterioration of saturated, or nearly saturated, wood.

Dry rot or fungal damage to wood. Thrives in the presence of moisture. Under ideal conditions, which include darkness, poor ventilation and wood that has a moisture content of at least 20 percent, irreparable dry rot damage due to fungi can occur in as little as three months.

Insect damage to wood. More likely to occur when the wood is damp.

Rust, the corrosion of iron and steel. Needs high humidity to occur. The more moisture is present, the faster rust develops.

Galvanic corrosion, the deterioration of metal when two different metals are in contact. Electrochemical action occurs on the surface in the presence of moisture. This condition is unlikely in very dry climates.

Foundation slippage and failure. Often caused by excess ground water.

Masonry and mortar deterioration. Hastened by the effects of acid rain, which contains pollutants such as sulfuric acid. Especially vulnerable are limestone, marble, sandstone and brownstone, which are destroyed as a result of their contact with the acid. The effect of the pollutants on the masonry is also sometimes called "stone disease."

Spalling and delamination of masonry. Occur most often as a direct result of the presence of moisture in the stone, brick, block, stucco or concrete. This process occurs more quickly in areas subject to frequent winter freeze-thaw cycles.

Premature paint failure. Traced in most cases to the presence of moisture in the material to which the paint has been applied.

Dry rot damage caused by a clogged drainage system, affecting both the structure and the exterior cladding of the building.

Sandstone deterioration, due in part to atmospheric pollution. The poor patching is also contributing to the destruction of the columns.

historic material that has survived, thereby avoiding the necessity of a replacement element.

- Paint or stain, as appropriate, unprotected wood, iron and steel in order to protect these materials from the elements.

- Resist the temptation to cover up deterioration with metal, vinyl or other nonhistoric materials.

- Replace missing or badly deteriorated features or parts of them with matching elements.

FOUNDATIONS

In making structural repairs, work on the foundation first. Without a sound base, the viability of the entire building is at risk. If you are unsure of the structural stability of your house's foundation, have it professionally examined and any necessary repairs made. Here a second opinion is a good idea, particularly if the remedy recommended is costly or drastic. Foundations, probably more than any other area of a building, receive "preservation treatments" galore, many of which do little or nothing to preserve the house and some of which actually cause damage.

A common reason for deterioration of foundations is the continued presence of water, usually because of a site drainage problem. Moisture, rising up through the masonry foundation and walls by capillary action, deposits on or beneath the surface dissolved salts, known as efflorescence or subflorescence. Installing a damp-proof course, or waterproof membrane, in the foundation will prevent the water from rising, but this procedure is more common in very wet climates and rarely used in the United States. To correct the problem, the ground must slope away from the foundation so that ground water is directed away. If the problem is severe, you could consider installing a site drainage system.

Do not worry about every small crack or minor fissure in the house's foundation. A professional inspection will usually help put your mind at ease, so have one done if you are at all concerned. Cracks can be monitored by periodic photographs or by special measuring devices.

Rising damp, caused by poor site drainage, in a c. 1840 brick house. Not only has the moisture saturated the brick above the stone foundation, it has dissolved much of the mortar between bricks.

Do not attempt to solve a foundation problem by covering it with a coating or another material. In addition to not providing a solution to the problem, the cover-up may hide or even hasten further deterioration. Replace damaged or missing foundation materials with ones that match the originals and repoint the masonry, if necessary (see page 142).

If you find you need to alter the foundation, get professional advice before removing any portion of a foundation to install a window or other opening and make sure proper support is provided for the structure above the new opening, both temporarily and permanently. Likewise, when repairing a foundation, make provisions for support-

Right: Structural failure caused by removing a section of the foundation without supporting the wall above in order to create a basement entrance.

Below: Structural repair of masonry by dismantling and rebuilding the failed wall. (Joel Snyder)

PREVENTING WOOD DETERIORATION

Problem	Cause	Cure
Abrasion	Foot traffic; rubbing from furniture and hardware; abrasive cleaning	Protect wood in high-traffic areas with floor coverings; paint wood; avoid harsh stripping and cleaning methods.
Scorching, burning	Heat from stoves, lights	Protect wood from exposure to heat sources.
Insects	Termites, carpenter ants, carpenter bees, woodwasps, powder post beetles, deathwatch beetles	Exterminate; treat wood members; ventilate, dehumidify to reduce moisture.
Dry rot, mold, mildew	Fungus	Treat with fungicide; ventilate, dehumidify, provide light to deter growth.
Wet rot	Water	Remove water sources; provide good drainage and ventilation; dry out wood; protect end grain.
Mechanical or structural failure	Improper use such as forcing windows and doors to open and close; too much weight on floors or roof; poor design	Realign to facilitate movement between parts; have structural capacity and stability analyzed; remove heavy loads; provide necessary support.

ing the wall above the area where you are working. Professional advice will also be required for alterations such as installing seismic anchors to help prevent earthquake damage; here you will also need to know local requirements.

Trees and shrubs growing close to the house should be

removed, and new trees and shrubs should be planted well away from the foundation. The root systems of trees and other foundation plantings can threaten the structure by holding moisture at or near the foundation and by robbing clay soil of its moisture thus opening up voids in the soil. These voids encourage foundation settlement and can lead to severe damage. Climbing or vining plants growing up the foundation and walls of the house can cause damage by holding moisture against the building and secreting acids that damage building materials. Cut them off at the ground, then gently pull the vines and leaves away from the wall once they have died. If you do not remove the roots, however, the vines are likely to grow back in a short time.

Make sure the foundation is ventilated by special vents through the wall into crawl spaces or by operable windows. To allow light and air to reach the foundation, relocate any items such as logs, bricks and tools that are located at or near the foundation.

Permanently filled-in basement windows blocking air circulation and light from basements and crawl spaces.

WALLS

For most historic houses, the walls are the most visible single feature, establishing the historic character and style of the building. Constructed of wood, masonry, earth or metal and covered with an amazing variety of historic materials, their preservation is essential to the continued viability of the house.

As with all parts of the house, retain the exterior appearance of the walls by repairing and retaining not only the main surfaces but also the trim, such as window and door surrounds, corner boards and decorative masonry. When repairing old stucco finishes, use a stucco mix and finishing technique that matches the original as closely as possible.

Follow professional advice on how to correct a wall that is bowing or leaning or appears to be in danger of collapsing. Such problems can often be solved without rebuilding the wall, thereby saving money and historic materials. In

Cover-up. The removal of original features and installation of aluminum siding on this house have contributed significantly to the loss of historic character.

Above: Bricked-in door opening, disrupting the historical appearance and characteristic symmetry of this double house.

Opposite: Carefully repaired and preserved siding and wood trim. The house's original architectural character has been preserved.

such cases, it is wise to get more than one opinion. Tie rods provide structural stability to any house and should not be tampered with.

In masonry construction, replace irreparably damaged bricks, stones or blocks with ones that match in appearance and composition. Do not assume that old mortar needs to be replaced. Repoint mortar joints only if the mortar is missing or deeply weathered. Use a lime-sand mortar mix that matches the original in composition and appearance by having the original mortar analyzed. If repointing must be done, finish the joints in the same way as the originals, usually recessed slightly. Modern, hard cement mortars are not compatible with old masonry and, because they are harder than brick or stone, will not contract in periods of freezing and thawing, thus causing the masonry to deteriorate. Avoid sealing masonry walls with a water-repellent coating. This procedure may cause, not solve, problems.

If the original wood siding is missing or beyond repair in wood construction, investigate to determine the cause of the deterioration, solve the problem, repair any structural damage and use replacement wood siding that is the same width and profile as the original. If only one area of the siding is damaged, replace the siding only in that area. Resist the temptation to install aluminum or vinyl siding or other cover-up material, as these will change the appearance of the house and may mask deterioration. Remember that cover-up materials often make a house less attractive to potential buyers.

Wood siding and trim with peeling paint should be properly prepared for a new coat of paint after correcting the problem, then repainted (see pages 156–59). Before repainting, check joints between different surfaces and materials, replacing damaged or missing caulking, if necessary. If peeling paint and deteriorating siding are caused by blown-in insulation installed in the wall cavity without a vapor barrier, you can reduce the interior moisture by installing vented plugs on the exterior.

Tree or shrub branches that brush against the walls should be trimmed.

CLEANING BUILDINGS GENTLY

Beauty truly is in the eye of the beholder. Nearly everyone has a different idea of what looks good. Some people, in fact, admire the aged patina of old dirty brick, stone, wood and other materials and believe a building that is old should look that way. Others feel that any surface that appears dirty should be cleaned.

First, ask yourself why you want to clean the house. Remember that you will very likely damage the building if you want to have a brand-new look, which may not be achievable anyway. You probably want to clean the building to make it look better, not preserve it. Only in rare cases does surface dirt damage a building. For these reasons and because this undertaking is hardly ever inexpensive or simple, the cleaning of any masonry, wood or metal surfaces solely to make them look better should not be a high priority.

Many homeowners, in an effort to let everyone know

Above: Old brick with a historic patina. Note the original narrow mortar joints.

Left: Sandblasted brick. Note that the texture and once-crisp corner have been altered.

that work on the house has started, hasten first to clean the exterior masonry or wood siding by the method that seems easiest and least expensive. In some areas this method is sandblasting, waterblasting, wire brushing or burning to remove paint from wood siding. Be aware that each method is harmful to the historic fabric. On a masonry building such cleaning can remove a hard outer surface and expose a previously protected soft inner core to the elements. It also destroys the surface texture, stone tooling marks, sculptural treatments and corners. Abrasive cleaning of wood can permanently change its texture, and hence its appearance, raise the grain and make it unreceptive to paint or other finishes. Abrasive cleaning of metal can destroy protective galvanization (zinc coating), remove plated metal coatings and pit and alter the surface texture.

If you do decide to clean, the gentlest method of cleaning is usually a light scrubbing with a soft bristle brush and water. This method, similar to that for cleaning interior plaster walls, removes the surface dirt and residue, but does not harm the masonry, mortar or wood. If only a small area

Before and after gentle cleaning. Only the dirt is gone on the left, and the mortar and brick texture have not been affected by the detergent cleaning.

needs to be cleaned of dirt or paint, clean only that area and leave the rest of the building alone.

If you want to remove paint from a masonry surface, you need to do some homework to determine why the paint was applied in the first place. If the house was painted when it was originally built, then the paint is a historic feature, and the house should be repainted after careful surface preparation.

If the paint was applied later, or even originally, it was probably done to protect the masonry, hide mismatched stone or brick or mask changes. If you decide to remove paint, use a product specifically formulated for use on the material you are cleaning. These products are often applied in poultice form, then rinsed off with low-pressure water

Mottled effect on brick left by acid burn. Caused by improper chemical cleaning, this condition is irreversible.

147

Bricks repointed with a modern mortar mix with a high portland cement content. As a result of expansion and contraction, the bricks are being crushed, since they are so much softer than the mortar.

after softening the paint. With any cleaning process involving chemicals, collect the residue and dispose of it properly.

If you need to remove built-up paint from wood siding or shingles, consider using an electric heat plate on flat areas or a heat gun. Take precautions to avoid exposure to lead and to prevent fires. You may be able to do a good job by lightly scraping and then sanding the areas where paint still remains, feathering paint layers out where they meet the bare wood. The latter methods work best when the paint remaining on the siding or shingles is minimal.

Any cleaning method you are considering should be tested in an appropriate place, such as the rear wall, before you start the job. Do the test cleaning at least a month before you start the actual cleaning, so you have ample time to study the results and make decisions accordingly.

Beware of masonry cleaning processes that include chemicals, whether in proprietary formulas or not. Chemical cleaning, contrary to popular belief, can be very damaging to the house and can cause permanent destruction, discoloration and staining of masonry. Some chemical cleaners are effective, but others are not. Do not, for example, use hydrochloric (muriatic) acid to clean dirty masonry and avoid cleaning limestone or marble with an acidic cleaner.

Steer clear of any cleaning method that could be abrasive. Some damage to the surface of the material being cleaned might occur, and you don't want to take chances. Remember that anything under enough pressure, even plain water, will be abrasive. A water pressure of less than 300 psi (pounds per square inch) is suggested for cleaning. Remember, too, that abrasive damage to masonry, wood or metal is irreversible.

Do not assume that if you clean masonry you will need to repoint the mortar joints. If the mortar was in good condition before gentle cleaning, repointing should not be necessary.

Avoid sealing any masonry surface with a water-repellent coating. These silicone, acrylic and other coatings will not permit liquid water to escape from the wall but will allow water vapor in. The water vapor condenses at cold spots in the wall and freezes in cold climates, which can cause the masonry to spall — that is, to flake so that its face cracks and falls off. This condition can also cause moisture damage to interior surfaces. In other words, if you have used the gentlest effective method for cleaning the building, you will be wasting your money and putting the house in danger by applying a sealer.

WINDOWS AND DOORS

Treat the windows as one of the most important features of your historic house. The sensitive treatment of historic windows and doors is one key to a successful rehabilitation project, both aesthetically and physically. Whether your windows are wood double-hung sash, steel casements with leaded glass or any other type, they are important. Significant elements of every window are the overall size, design and details, method of operation, materials and the planes of the frame, sash and glass. If you must make repairs to the old windows or, as a last resort, install new ones, avoid changing the appearance not only of the sash, but also of the window details, such as the exterior and interior frames, lintels, sills, hoodmolds and hardware. Some windows on the market include

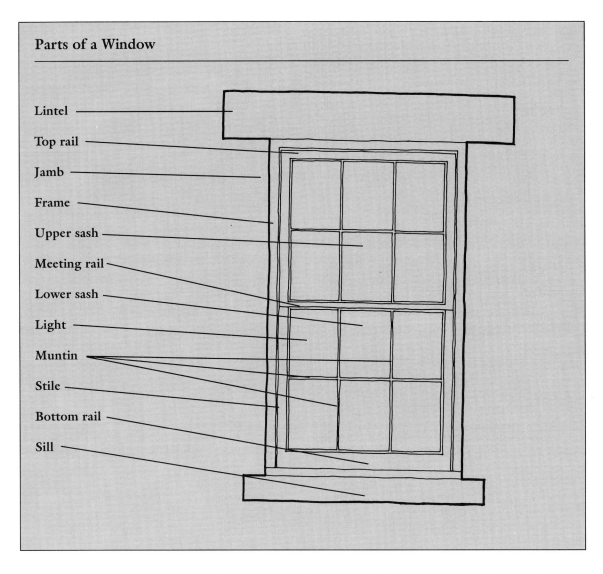

Parts of a Window

Lintel
Top rail
Jamb
Frame
Upper sash
Meeting rail
Lower sash
Light
Muntin
Stile
Bottom rail
Sill

between-the-glass or applied muntins. Avoid using them, as they will not match original windows and not many people will be fooled into thinking that the windows have true divided sash.

Replace only the parts of a window or a door that are missing or too deteriorated to save. If the sill has disintegrated because of dry rot, for example, do not assume that the rest of the window is also beyond repair. Consider rebuilding deteriorated sash or frames, replacing or consolidating with epoxy those parts that are badly rotted or otherwise damaged. Do not rely solely on appearance to de-

Types of Windows

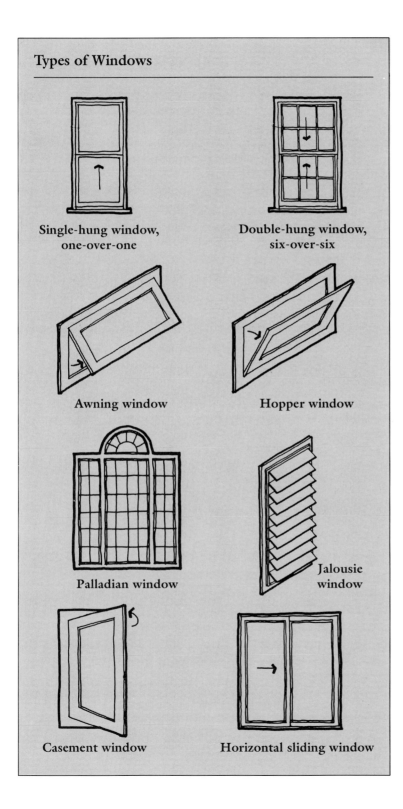

Single-hung window,
one-over-one

Double-hung window,
six-over-six

Awning window

Hopper window

Palladian window

Jalousie
window

Casement window

Horizontal sliding window

Above left: Repairable window that can serve for many more years, particularly if it is protected by a compatible exterior storm window.

Above right: Replacement window with false-appearing, between-the-glass "sandwich" muntins, not a recommended treatment.

termine if an entire window or door needs to be replaced.

If windows are missing or have been insensitively replaced, conduct research to determine the original appearance of windows. If your research turns up nothing, then use replacements based on the appearance of historic windows and doors on buildings of similar type, style, date and location.

Consider also the following points as you evaluate your windows and doors:

■ Protect historic window sash and save energy at the same time by installing compatible exterior storm sash (see page 165).

- The placement of skylights can be problematical. These seemingly harmless additions can have a major effect on the exterior appearance of the house.

- Exterior shutters are not appropriate for every historic house, and, when they are appropriate, they should be operable and fit properly, covering the opening completely when closed. Only since the 1950s have shutters come into use as decorative features.

- Do not block or fill in, even partially, an original or historic window or door opening on a major elevation of the house. If you do fill in a rear opening, make the change easily reversible and maintain the exterior appearance.

Skylights. Even a small addition can be visually damaging to a historic house, as demonstrated by the skylight on the front roof slope of the house to the left. The house on the right also has a skylight, but it is hidden behind a dormer. On this house, however, the replacement roofing material, with its mottled appearance, does not resemble the original slate.

153

ROOFS, GUTTERS AND DOWNSPOUTS

The roof is the house's first defense against wind, rain, snow and ice. Its original form, details and materials are significant to the architectural and historic character of every house. For these reasons, approach any rehabilitation work to the roof with extreme caution. If you have concerns about the structural stability of all or part of the roof, seek professional assistance and correct any problems that are found. Most early roofing materials, including wood shakes and shingles, metal, clay tile and slate, are still available today, and the techniques and tools for installing them are known. In addition, some replacements are excellent and do a good job of reproducing the appearance, if not the material, of the original roofs.

In making repairs, respect the form and details of the historic roof, gutters and downspouts by not removing historic features, even if you believe they have no function other than decoration. If they are deteriorated, repair and retain them, avoiding covering them with aluminum or vinyl. If they must be replaced, use the type and profile of gutter that is correct for the style of your house and appropriate for the form of the roof. Use extreme caution if you are planning to add a dormer to a roof for more living space. An addition of inappropriate size or style will destroy the character of your historic house (see page 159).

Remember that downspouts, in order to function well, must run all the way to the ground and end well away from the foundation, draining water away from the house. In addition, a splash block or other device can be installed below the downspout to direct water away.

The roof must be properly ventilated to prevent problems caused by ice and snow dams and icicles. Consider installing electric heating cables to prevent ice and snow dams if you have short lengths of gutters or if the design of your roof is complex. Use original gable, soffit and roof vents for their intended purpose. Do not block them or install a fixed window or panel behind them. Install unobtrusive vents in the attic if none exists (see page 182).

Retain and repair the historic roofing material, if at all possible. It is far better to use all the good slate, metal or tile on the most visible slopes of the roof, reroofing only

Water damage. Ice dams, here formed at the eaves of an uninsulated or poorly ventilated roof when melted snow refroze, can cause water to back up into the attic resulting in destruction of eaves, gutters and downspouts.

the rest, for example, than to remove all the roofing and proceed to reroof the entire house. If you must reroof all or part of the house, be certain that the type, texture and color of replacement roofing you use is appropriate. Look at actual installations of the replacement roofing you are considering using before you make your decision. It is extremely hazardous, and in most parts of the country it is illegal, to install new roofing over a series of old roofs or over deteriorated sheathing. Make repairs instead.

Replace or repair missing or deteriorated flashing. Flashing, usually made of metal, should be installed at every place where two different materials or surfaces meet such as at the base of the chimney or between the edge of the roof and the gutter. As mentioned earlier, prevent two different metals from coming in contact with each other to avoid galvanic corrosion.

Chimneys and parapets need special attention and should be repaired.

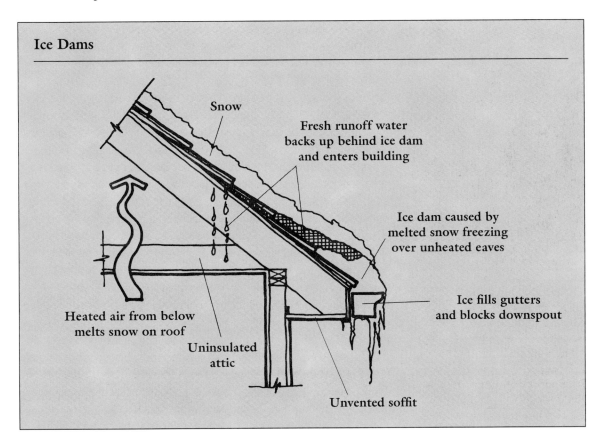

Ice Dams

Snow

Fresh runoff water backs up behind ice dam and enters building

Ice dam caused by melted snow freezing over unheated eaves

Ice fills gutters and blocks downspout

Heated air from below melts snow on roof

Uninsulated attic

Unvented soffit

PAINTING

Paint has two purposes: to protect and preserve the material to which it is applied, primarily the role of exterior paint, and to provide decorative effects, the chief role of interior paint. Historic layers of paint, important physical evidence of the house's past, are as significant an element as any other and must be treated carefully.

The common paints in this country have always been water or oil based, but today's latex and alkyd (synthetic resin) paints are quite different from the early whitewashes, distemper and linseed oil–based formulas. In the late 19th and early 20th centuries, in particular, sanded paints and other textured finishes were popularly used to imitate stone or other materials. Stenciling, graining, marbleizing and other special techniques were, and are, used to achieve special effects, and these finishes are extremely important character-defining features, particularly for house interiors.

You can begin by investigating the house's historic paint colors and application techniques as well as the relationship of one color to another. This project can be fun and requires nothing more than a knife, some sandpaper and lots of patience! Expose the layers of paint present on the house, particularly in corners and other areas where paint buildup is likely to have occurred and where the surfaces have been protected from sunlight. To do this research, make a wide V-cut in the surface, down to the base material, scrape and carefully sand the cut until it is three or more inches wide. You will then have all of the paint layers, and the dirt layers between them, exposed and ready for examination with a hand magnifier. You will want to repeat this procedure for all parts of the building that were painted. An alternative is to examine the paint layers of a removed sample under a low-power stereoscopic microscope.

Knowledge of the composition of the existing paint can be important, as some types of paint do not bond well with others. For example, modern latex paint will not adhere well to old oil-based paint, causing a significant percentage of the paint failures in old houses today. Resist the temptation to use many different colors to enhance wood details,

Unpainted exterior masonry getting a paint job, not a recommended treatment in this case. If the masonry has not been painted and is in good condition, painting is unnecessary. (Glenn A. Harper)

unless your investigation revealed that this approach is historically correct. Otherwise, you may create your own architectural folly.

Work carefully on surface preparation, the most important part of the painting process. You will be wasting money and time if you attempt to apply new coats of paint over peeling, blistering, poorly adhering or extremely thick layers of old paint. Simply face the fact that it may be necessary to remove most, if not all, of the old exterior paint. If you find it is not necessary to undertake a major paint re-

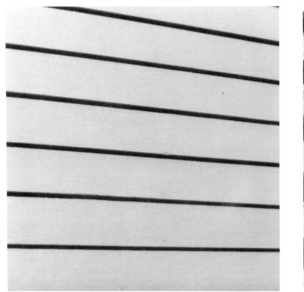

Above left: Good surface preparation and recent re-painting of wood siding.

Above right: New paint, failing after only three months. Poor surface preparation is the cause. Before further painting, all the old, and new, paint will need to be removed.

moval project, be sure the surface is sound, that any old paint remaining is securely attached to the base material and that the surface is clean and has an even "tooth" to which the new paint can adhere. Cross-grain cracking, checking and alligatoring are all problems caused by improper surface preparation.

Removing paint from any surface can be a time-consuming, tedious task but well worth your efforts if the surface has severely deteriorated. Special care must be taken with masonry surfaces where paint often has been applied to protect inferior or soft brick. Abrasive removal could easily remove the surface of this brick. Such surfaces will need a new coat of paint. In other cases, you may uncover unsightly or badly deteriorated surfaces, which will force you to repaint in any case. In removing paint, every effort should be made to protect workers by ensuring they are well clothed and purchasing and using respirators. Keep children well away from the working area, because many historic paints contain lead.

Paint should be removed preferably with heat methods or chemical strippers and not by open-flame methods such as propane torches. More than one historic house has been heavily damaged or destroyed by a fire started during a paint removal project. Of course, all heat methods including electric heat plates and guns can also cause fires, and some chemical removers are both toxic and flammable. Do not use abrasive, and therefore destructive, paint removal methods, such as wire brushing or sandblasting. (See more about removing paint on pages 147–48.)

If you are painting dried-out bare wood that has not been painted for some time, such as a window frame, consider brushing surfaces with boiled linseed oil before applying an oil-based or alkyd paint. The oil will soak into the wood and help to preserve it. Always use primers and paint that are specifically formulated for use on the material you are painting — masonry paint for masonry, metal paint for metal and so forth.

Paint adheres best when the temperature is between 40° to 90°F and the prepared surface is neither too hot nor too cold. Do not apply paint to surfaces in direct sunlight, for example. Finally, avoid beginning a paint job if rain is expected.

ADDITIONS

Whether you are planning to install a small skylight or dormer, or construct a multiroom addition, weigh carefully the visual and economic effect your project will have on the house and its neighborhood. In many cases, additions actually lower the value of the house or make it less attractive to potential buyers. You may have a house for which virtually any addition would be visually disastrous. Too many homeowners come to this realization only after they have finished their additions.

On the other hand, your house may already include an addition. Do not assume that you will need to remove this during your rehabilitation project. It may be significant historically and architecturally and also provide additional needed space for you. Conduct a careful evaluation before deciding on a course of action.

If you feel that the house can accommodate an addition without damage to its historic and architectural character, study carefully the massing and proportions of your house and its neighbors and respect these in the placement, size and design of the addition. This is not an easy task. It requires a high degree of sensitivity and design ability to ar-

Historic home before and after construction of an addition. Note that the addition appears to be a separate building, so the original house retains its historic form.

rive at a solution that will respect, but not copy, the original building and that clearly will be subordinate to it.

Enclosing a historic open porch by putting fixed walls between the columns or posts will alter, if not destroy, the massing and proportions of the house. If you do decide to enclose a porch, consider making the enclosing elements entirely removable or, at least, making them appear as if they are easily removable. Similarly, changing a roof to install a deck, dormer or visible skylight will have a negative effect on the house's overall appearance.

Unless you are authentically reconstructing an early addition, porch or other feature using actual physical and visual evidence, do not attempt to make an addition look as if it has always been there. Copying a historical prototype that did not exist on the site is rarely successful in fooling anyone, and it creates a false sense of history, undermining the significance of the historic house. Use details that are clearly different from, but compatible with, the historic ones.

Here are some factors to consider:

■ Research the applicable zoning restrictions in your area before finalizing the conceptual design.

■ Use compatible materials and colors in the addition, avoiding any treatment that would draw undue attention to the addition and away from the historic house.

■ Consider constructing an addition that appears to be a freestanding building separate from the original structure. This approach works particularly well for smaller houses.

■ Be particularly sensitive when adding a deck to a historic house. Such additions often have a character completely different from that of the house and tend to draw quite a bit of attention to themselves.

Landscaping and Outbuildings

Historic landscape features should be regarded as significant elements of the house — as significant as the form of the roof, the design of the porch or the arrangement of rooms.

In addition to original planting beds, hedgerows, shrubs and trees, your house inspection also may reveal historic features such as retaining walls, fences, paved areas, walk-

Above: Early farm-industry complex, now increasingly rare. Included are the house, a large barn and the ruins of a sawmill to the right of the house. Here, preservation of the setting and the relationship of the buildings to one another are of vital importance to the study and understanding of how these early complexes worked.

Right: Alley lined with historic barns, carriage houses and garages, all of which are important to the preservation of this historic residential district.

ways, wells and cisterns. Historic outbuildings can include carriage houses and garages, privies, barns of all types, springhouses and tool sheds. Such secondary structures, as they are called, are, in reality, often as important as the house itself, and in some cases more so, possibly because of their rarity or unaltered condition. Treat these structures with the same care and study that you give to the house itself. You may be able to adapt an old and historic outbuilding to a new use. For instance, an old barn could become a garage or guest quarters or even a separate apartment. Be sure to check your local zoning regulations first.

If you cannot preserve a historic outbuilding where it is located, as a last resort, consider moving it to another part of the lot or to a nearby location. Perhaps someone else in your historic neighborhood could put the building to good use.

Before any change to your site and outbuildings occurs, be sure you've considered the following recommendations:

- Arrange, if possible, for an archeological assessment of the property, particularly if you have reason to believe that

Garage from the 1920s with its original doors maintained and preserved, a new roof and aluminum siding. While the use of aluminum siding is not recommended, at least this garage, which is not in a historic district, can easily be returned to its original appearance. Sometimes such compromises are necessary.

Garden of an Italian Villa house with spare plantings near the house's foundations. The circular garden in front of the house was a popular element in Victorian domestic landscapes. (NTHP)

prehistoric or historic features remain below the ground. When planting flowers or shrubs, for example, you may have found the remains of a brick or stone foundation.

■ Be aware that foundation plantings are not only historically incorrect for many houses, they also can damage the building (see pages 139–40).

■ Avoid an incompatible landscape treatment in a public location. A large rock garden in front of one house whose neighbors have original grassy lawns may diminish the historic character of the entire street.

■ Exercise restraint in installing other landscape features, such as fountains, pools or gazebos that may be out of character or out of scale with the historic house.

ENERGY CONSERVATION

The sensible use of energy is everyone's concern and responsibility. Regardless of how much money you have, you certainly do not want to waste it by heating and cooling the air above and around your house. Historic features of the house, such as porches and overhangs, are not just decorative, they have important energy-saving functions as well.

Here are some ways to conserve energy around your old house:

Plantings around the house provide important energy options. Shade trees, which lose their leaves in the fall, can save energy dollars in the summer, especially on a sunny side of the house. Evergreen trees act as a windbreak in the winter on exposed sides of the house. If you live in a hot climate, the value of well-placed trees cannot be overstated. Any trees or shrubs should be planted well away from the house's foundation, however.

Storm windows and doors prevent actual air infiltration. Install compatible storm windows and doors that do not hide but can protect the historic features.

Caulking at the intersection of two different surfaces or materials, such as between a window frame and the siding or masonry wall, also prevents air from reaching the interior. Also, install weatherstripping under and around moving parts, such as exterior doors and windows.

About Storm Windows

Installing storm windows on an old house can help considerably in saving energy costs. The storm windows should be as unobtrusive as possible, drawing no attention to themselves. Here are a few tips to follow.

- Ensure they are compatible in color with the exterior of the house.

- Make or purchase storm windows that are the same size and configuration as the primary windows. For double-hung sash, the meeting rail, located where the upper and lower sash meet, should be in the same location as in the primary sash.

- Install them on the outside of the house to protect the historic primary sash. If you install storm windows on the interior, you will force the house's historic windows to serve as storm sash. Nevertheless, in a few cases, interior installation is preferable, especially when the decorative appearance of original windows would be hidden or damaged by exterior storm windows.

INSIDE THE OLD HOUSE

Historic interiors are sometimes considered of secondary importance to historic exteriors. This mistaken notion is reinforced by the wording of most local historic preservation laws, which concentrate on exteriors with the possibility of only an occasional review of an outstanding historic public interior. The imbalance between interest in the preservation and sensitive treatment of exteriors versus interiors has begun to be addressed. A major national conference and exposition on historic interiors of all types sponsored by the National Park Service was held in 1988 in Philadelphia, and publications on how to rehabilitate historic interior materials and features are increasing.

It is true that exteriors must be properly maintained to provide basic protection for interiors, and that interiors must, perhaps by necessity, be adjusted somewhat to suit the particular needs of the occupants at the time of their tenancy. But it must be acknowledged that historic interior room arrangements, relationships and proportions, as well as original details that are simply unavailable in houses built today, are exciting, interesting and worth adapting ourselves to, rather than the other way around. People who grew up in old and historic houses usually have no trouble with high ceilings, small bathrooms and little closet space! In other words, such features are not intrinsically negative — they are simply different from what people have become accustomed to and what is generally available in houses built today.

Opposite: Dining room of Stan Hywet Hall, 1915, the Tudor Revival mansion and estate of the Seiberling family of Akron, Ohio, and now a restored house museum. Work on the house continues as research leads to new information about the house's past. (Walter Long)

Top and above: Fireplace in a bedroom at The Georgian, Lancaster, Ohio, before and after restoration. The chair rail was reconstructed and the wall patched with new plaster and painted.

The Secretary of the Interior's Standards for Rehabilitation (see page 32) apply to interior as well as exterior work. This chapter covers the points to consider in the sensitive and sensible rehabilitation of historic house interiors and offers basic rehabilitation advice.

INTERIOR MATERIALS AND FEATURES

Assessing interior features. The early electric lighting fixture in the ceiling and historic mantel in this bedroom can be saved. The wallpaper has been damaged beyond repair, while sections of baseboard that do not match exactly indicate that one wall is not original. (Rita Walsh)

Wood and plaster are by far the most common interior building materials used in historic houses throughout the United States. Common finishing materials include paint, wallpaper and ceramic tile, but masonry, metals, glass, linoleum, fabric, pressed paper and tooled leather also have been used in old houses. Special materials, including scagliola (plaster painted to look like stone), and techniques, such as grain-

Problems Caused by Moisture

Damage to windows, plaster and other interior materials and finishes is often caused by condensation occurring on surfaces where cold, dry outside air meets warm, humid inside air. Lack of a vapor barrier and inadequate ventilation often lead to these conditions. Other interior deterioration problems, caused either directly or indirectly by moisture, follow:

Cracking, powdering and failing plaster. Often the result of damaged roofing, flashing, gutters and downspouts.

Mold and mildew, with their musty odors. Flourish in dark, poorly ventilated spaces where moisture is present.

Blistering and peeling paint and wallpaper. Can indicate poor roof drainage and that water is getting into the building through gaps in flashing, caulking, weatherstripping or mortar.

Stained, swelling and cracking woodwork. Can result from plumbing leaks or any of the causes mentioned previously.

Dry rot, insect damage to wood. Abetted by the presence of moisture.

Discoloration, dry rot, wet rot. Possibly caused by leaking pipes and air-conditioning units.

Floor stains, dry rot. Can be caused by overwatering plants or by simple carelessness in mopping up spills or rainwater.

---

ing to give softwood the appearance of a more expensive hardwood, are more frequently found in interiors where materials do not have to withstand the elements and dramatic changes in temperature.

The most common features that define the character of historic house interiors are woodwork, mantelpieces, stairways, windows, doors, transoms, decorative plaster, built-in cabinets, light fixtures, radiators, plumbing fixtures and hardware. Do not overlook the importance of such seemingly trivial or mundane items as the height and profile of the baseboards, the configuration of door and window frames, kitchen and pantry cabinets and ceramic tile-covered floors and walls. All help to define the character of the interior.

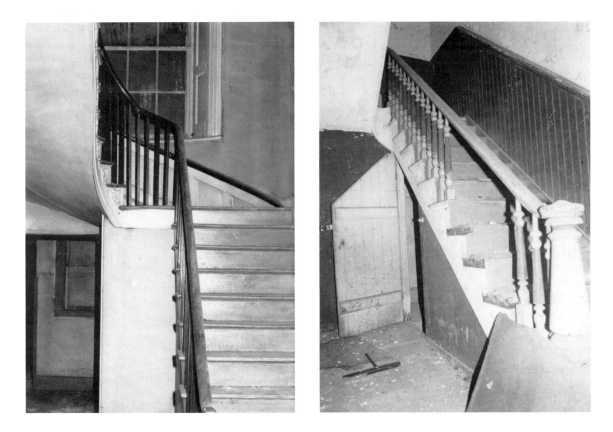

Two stairways. The early 19th-century stairway on the left is well preserved because the exterior of the house has been carefully maintained over the years. That on the right requires only simple repairs: replacing the missing balusters with matching pieces, repairing the wood and plaster, then repainting. (Ohio Historic Preservation Office)

If a home lacks these character-defining features, you may be tempted to install, for instance, molding or a baseboard salvaged from other buildings. If your research does not reveal what the house's missing historic features looked like, it would be preferable not to install these features at all or to install contemporary features that are compatible with the historic style and character of the house.

Stairways often are a dominant feature in an old-house interior. Closing up open stairways and opening closed ones are not recommended in any rehabilitation. On the one hand, you will be changing the relationship of the stairway to the remainder of the house, and on the other, you run the risk of completely changing the historic character of the interior by making what was perhaps a secondary stairway into a focal point.

Any interior changes should be reversible. For example, you may live in a house that has a historic mantelpiece you do not like. Instead of removing the mantel, you could cover it with a plasterboard box, removing it at the time you decide

to sell the property. The new owners may love the mantel!

On the other hand, if you wish to use a historic fireplace, be sure to have it inspected for safety. At a minimum the chimney will need to be cleaned, and you may have to install a flue liner and a damper.

Here are some specific items to be aware of:

■ Identify potentially dangerous materials that are present in your house, have them evaluated and, if necessary, removed. Examples of these are friable asbestos and flaking lead paint.

■ Identify and be particularly careful with finishes, primarily on wood but also on other materials. You may think you are dealing with oak or walnut, for example, but it may be pine painted and grained to look like oak or walnut. Graining woodwork has been a common procedure throughout the history of this country, so be careful if you are planning to strip paint or varnish from woodwork in an effort to refinish it.

Above left and right: Examples of wood graining from the Gallier House, New Orleans. Some techniques of graining are more painterly than others and can be detected easily. Others simulate wood grain so expertly, it can be difficult to tell which is wood and which graining. (Bill van Calsem)

BASEMENTS AND CRAWL SPACES

One of the most common problems in old houses (and new houses, for that matter) is water in the basement. This situation is often the result of poor drainage from the site or from the roof or paved areas around the house. The basements of old houses need not be damp, humid places. In fact, with good ventilation and drainage, they can be dry and quite comfortable.

One of the first projects you may consider for a basement or crawl space is to insulate. Insulate the basement and crawl spaces carefully, always placing a continuous vapor barrier on the heated side of the insulation, using the recommended thickness of insulation for your geographical area. Be certain that any excess moisture problems are corrected before installing insulation between the ceiling joists, with the vapor barrier facing up toward the first floor, for crawl spaces and unheated basements. In heated basements and furnace rooms, place insulation on the foundation walls, leaving a space between the insulation and the wall for ventilation. In this case, the vapor barrier should face in, toward the room, and the insulation should stop at a point about two feet below the frost line. At the same time, install pipe and duct insulation and consider insulating your hot-water heater.

Effective ventilation is one of the most important concerns to address in any old-house rehabilitation effort, and it is essential in basements and crawl spaces. Ventilate well, by opening windows or vents during both summer and winter, to allow outside air to circulate on the unheated side of any insulation. In addition, remove all items stored against the walls in the basement. This will allow you to inspect these walls all the way down to the floor and will permit air to circulate and dry out any moisture. Do not use the basement as a storage area.

Consider adopting the following recommendations as you work on your basement:

- Inspect the outside walls of the basement first, looking for signs of rising damp and blocked-up windows or vents. Remedy any drainage or other problems you find.

- Seek and follow professional advice in diagnosing and correcting any structural damage or deficiencies.

- Have your basement tested for the presence of radon gas, and take any necessary remedial measures.

- Have a professional pest inspection completed and correct any problems that exist. Do not forget to arrange for periodic follow-up inspections.

- Use a dehumidifier or two to reduce the amount of water vapor, directing the water to a basement drain, if you have one.

Installing a vapor barrier.
(Jack E. Boucher)

- Maintain a skeptical attitude toward any waterproof coatings you may be considering for the foundation of your house. If you have a very unusual situation that might warrant the application of a waterproof coating, first seek the advice of a professional and use the coating only in the areas that need it.

- Clear floor drains of any debris. If you live in an area with antiquated storm sewers, you may be faced with the problem of drain back-up during very hard rainstorms. Be prepared for this occurrence by raising appliances and other items well off the floor.

WALLS, CEILINGS AND FLOORS

Of great importance to the character of a historic house are the proportions of its spaces as determined by ceiling heights and room sizes. Also of significance are the placement of various spaces, the flow of the rooms (whether open or separated by walls and doors), the location of stairways, the types and location of historic trim and paneling and the presence of a wainscot in one or more rooms. All historic trim, wainscots, paneling and their finishes should remain in place. The design of the house will help you determine what changes can be made effectively and sensitively.

Do not remove or cover up any old trim, regardless of how plain it is, just for the sake of modernizing the house. If you want a completely modern interior, then purchase a recently built house. By retaining the trim and any paneling in place, a large part of the character of the interior will be preserved regardless of other changes you may make.

The material — often plaster or wood — and texture of the original ceilings and walls should be preserved. A modern substitute for flat plaster — plasterboard — has a slightly smoother, more regular surface than original plaster, but even this subtle change may be quite noticeable. Plasterboard patches with a plaster veneer are acceptable in many cases for repairing large areas of damaged or missing plaster, but use caution. Remember, too, that historically plaster was often meant to be covered by wallpaper or another material. In other words, when you expose plaster

that was meant to be wallpapered, you may be exposing a rough plaster finish that was not meant to be seen.

Wood is by far the most common flooring material, but tile, linoleum, floorcloths, mats and rugs of various types often have covered wood floors of old houses in the past. Owners of historic houses who love the beauty of old wood floors may plan to expose floors that may not have been exposed originally. But these floors, which are often made of pine or other softwood, deteriorate rapidly under use. Nothing is more beautiful than a nicely finished hardwood or softwood floor, but do not expect it to do more than it was meant to do. In other words, areas that were covered originally should continue to be covered. Generally, these areas include the center of the room and possibly the areas of heaviest traffic, including stairways.

Avoid covering original floors, walls or ceilings with inappropriate materials if you want a historic look. For exam-

Removing nonhistoric floor tiles from a pine floor in preparation for stripping and refinishing. In this case, the most difficult task was removing the adhesive that held the tile in place; an electric heat gun successfully took both paint and adhesive from the floor.

ple, do not put wall-to-wall carpeting over a decorative hardwood floor that was meant to be exposed. This, however, is a reversible action and would preserve the floor for another occupant who may want to expose it.

The following rehabilitation advice will help you rehabilitate your interior respectfully:

■ Removal and wholesale replacement of original plaster with plasterboard is rarely necessary. Similarly, covering plaster with plasterboard is unnecessary and creates problems at windows and doors. Remember how important it is to retain the historic materials. As with exterior surfaces, a cover-up approach rarely is a successful one.

■ If you must make minimal floor plan changes, be sure they are completely reversible. You house may be easier to sell and, in the event that you do not care for the results, it can easily be converted back to what it was originally.

■ Leave ceilings at their original heights. Ceiling height is an important design feature of most houses; if you lower the ceiling, you will instantly change the character of that room.

■ Be cautious about adding any new partitions or walls. Consider instead using screens or furniture as a room divider.

■ Install wood trim that is contemporary but compatible with the historic trim on any new walls you do erect. As with any addition to the building, you do not want to try to create an appearance that at first glance looks historic but is in fact something that never existed in that configuration historically. This type of approach undermines the significance of the actual historic features of the house.

■ Remember that small cracks in plaster surfaces are not necessarily a sign of trouble. If you decide to repair cracks to make the wall look better, you may need to enlarge them slightly to provide good adherence for the patching plaster.

■ Exercise caution on wallpaper removal, as steamers can be quite dangerous, and you may be destroying valuable evidence of the historic appearance of the house. Make an attempt to research the historic patterns for possible reproduction, if your goal is an authentic restoration.

■ Do not expose brick or stone that was originally plastered. Doing so will expose a rough masonry surface that was never meant to be exposed and will create a decidedly unoriginal and nonhistoric interior appearance.

- Remember that if you want to remove a section of floor to create a two-story space or a balcony, or to expose the structural details of a floor or roof, you are very likely violating the historic character of the house.

KITCHENS AND BATHROOMS

Kitchens and bathrooms pose the most difficult problems when rehabilitating a house, because these are the rooms many of us want most to change, to bring up to date. The best advice is to use common sense and respect the unique character of your historic house when contemplating changes to a kitchen or bathroom.

Kitchen in the Harriet Beecher Stowe House, 1871, Hartford, Conn., reflecting the author's theories about convenient and modern kitchens for the homemaker.

Bathroom, typical of many old houses. With some cosmetic work, this room could be very attractive. (Historic Preservation Associates)

In today's homes the kitchen is a popular place for gathering and socializing, a large space where everyone helps prepare a meal or at least observes its preparation. But this was not always the case. Victorian kitchens, for example, were generally out-of-the-way spaces occupied only by those who were actually cooking and serving the food.

Dual history revealed in a kitchen from the 1880s. The original wood wainscot, early upper cabinets and wood molding above the sink are from the late 19th century, while the tile, lower cabinets and sink, extending a few inches in front of the window, are from the 1950s. All this rehabilitation required was painting and the installation of a new floor.

Current ideas of what is appropriate for a kitchen or bathroom may not fit well with the house you occupy. Creating a large, open kitchen may require making drastic changes to the house. These will likely destroy significant spaces and features, and you may be very unhappy with the results. In some cases an addition may be more appropriate than the removal of interior walls. Similarly, adding or enlarging a bathroom may entail dividing a significant space or tearing up decorative wood and plaster features to install plumbing.

Kitchens and bathrooms should be well ventilated because of the moisture generated by the activities that occur there, particularly cooking and bathing. In fact, moisture problems throughout the house can be caused by one inadequately ventilated room that generates a lot of water vapor. If you have an old house whose kitchen or bathroom is not original, take particular care to study the results of the changes that were made when these rooms were installed or updated. For example, there may be signs of interior and exterior moisture damage as a result of poor ventilation, or water supply pipes may be located in areas that are particularly vulnerable to freezing.

Historic materials and features in the kitchen and bathroom such as plumbing fixtures, ceramic tile, old cabinets, decorative trim and wainscots should be retained and used, if possible. If your old house does not have these features, think carefully before deciding to install them. If you do decide to introduce some of these features into these rooms, do so in a contemporary but compatible manner. Also, do not assume that you need to remove kitchen and bathroom materials and features from the time those rooms were updated — say the 1940s, 1950s and 1960s. These periods also are, or are becoming, historic.

ATTICS

Attics of historic houses, because they are often exciting and beautiful spaces, are one of the first areas considered as new potential living space, especially as children's rooms; they are also popular as storage places. Expert repair of any structural problems, roof leaks and chimney deterioration, in addition to the proper installation of insulation and adequate ventilation, are essential projects that must be completed before any finishing of the attic is contemplated. As you rehabilitate the attic space, look for problem areas that may not show up until you or others actually begin working in the attic.

Insulate the attic before installing insulation in any

other location, since more heat loss and heat gain occur through the attic than any other location. If your attic will not be used as a living space, first place a continuous vapor barrier over and between the floor joists and then install insulation of the recommended thickness and type for your geographical area. If you intend to use the attic, install insulation below and between the rafters, leaving some space between the roof sheathing and the top of the insulation. Finish the project by installing a continuous vapor barrier

Typical old-house attic space, with good light from the frieze windows. This attic space could be rehabilitated to serve a variety of functions. (Ohio Historic Preservation Office)

on the heated, or inside, side of the insulation.

Outside air should circulate above this insulation. In case your house has no natural ventilation or historic vents, ventilation can be ensured by installing properly sized attic vents in the roof itself or in the soffits. The total area of the vents should be about $\frac{1}{150}$ of the square footage of the attic floor area. Therefore, for a floor area approximately 20 by 30 feet, or 600 square feet, the total ventilator area should be about 4 square feet (600 divided by 150). Four well-placed vents of 1 square foot each would do the job. Remember that the vents should be as visually unobtrusive as possible.

Here is some additional advice:

■ Use historic windows and vents for their originally intended functions of allowing air and light into the attic.

■ To avoid having to run ducts through the first floor, consider using your unused attic not only as a storage area but also as the location of the furnace for the second floor of the house.

■ Let caution guide you in making the decision to install skylights and in their placement. By putting a cardboard mock-up of the desired skylight on the roof and observing it from various locations, you will get some idea of how the installed skylight will appear.

■ Use even more caution in making the decision to build a dormer to create more living space. Do not, under any circumstances, build a dormer or dormers to create a second or third floor. Most new dormers have a dramatic, and usually detrimental, effect on the house's form and historic character.

HEATING, COOLING AND VENTILATION SYSTEMS

The mechanical systems of a historic house may be historic in their own right, and this possibility should be recognized in any rehabilitation effort. The old and historic radiators, ducts, grilles and registers add to the significance of the house. Equipment, however, does wear out and items such as boilers and furnaces may need to be replaced.

Do not assume that because your heating system is old,

it must be replaced with a new one. Have the entire system inspected, cleaned and repaired, if necessary, and continue to use it. The use of modern materials and technology, much of which can be successfully applied to older systems, also can make an old system more energy efficient.

If your house needs a new system, use a heating, cooling or ventilating system that has the least effect on the visual character of the house's interior. And avoid lowering ceilings or raising floors in order to accommodate any new system. Adding one, however, should present few difficulties. Today's systems are smaller and much less likely to intrude on historic features. For example, one contemporary heating system uses very small ducts that can be easily concealed. Locate any new ducts in already existing closets or secondary spaces, if possible.

Here are some other points:

■ Consider putting a furnace in the attic to serve the upper floor or floors of the house. This approach will eliminate the need for installing ductwork through the first floor thus causing physical and visual damage.

■ Avoid using a humidifier in a forced-air furnace so that damaging moisture will not be introduced into the house during cold months. Provide good ventilation for rooms of the house that have high humidity, such as kitchens and bathrooms.

PLUMBING AND ELECTRICAL SYSTEMS

Both water and gas pipes often run through historic houses. Even if you have installed a new system, unused pipes, if they are properly checked for leaks, then disconnected or capped, can remain in place without tearing up the house.

Your electrical needs depend largely on your lifestyle. Do you have lots of appliances and electrical equipment? Will a number of these be used by various family members at the same time? Do you have an electric clothes dryer? Consider reusing old plumbing and electrical fixtures, which are often of better quality than what is available today. Examples of these include light fixtures of all types, sinks, wash-

183

basins, toilets, utility tubs and bathtubs, which can be refinished, but often need nothing more than a good cleaning. Historic wall and ceiling light fixtures should not be removed, even though you may decide not to use them regularly.

While plumbing and electrical lines often must be updated in old houses, you should also take into account the following:

- Check the local plumbing and electrical codes or seek advice from your plumber or electrician before planning any work.

- Have a professional electrical inspection done if there is a question in your mind about the safety or adequacy of your system. Obtain advice on what type of service you should have.

- If you need additional electrical outlets, consider installing them in baseboards or other less visually intrusive locations. Electrical wiring can be hidden in or adjacent to existing moldings.

- Install and maintain battery-operated smoke alarms to cover all parts of your historic house, particularly the basement, attic, kitchen and stairways. Be certain that at least one alarm can be heard from each bedroom.

- Consider installing a security system if you feel that your particular situation warrants the expense.

ENERGY CONSERVATION

Crucial to the economical, efficient operation of your house is its low energy consumption. Some sensible, simple measures can result in significant savings for you.

Start with passive energy conservation measures inside. Open interior transoms; close doors; turn lights, heating and cooling down or off at night and limit their use in rooms not being used. Of course, you need to use common sense here to keep pipes from freezing and prevent potential damage to materials and finishes. Consider using bulbs of a low wattage where bright lights are not necessary.

Heating, cooling and ventilating systems should be inspected annually, and make it a habit to change or clean

ABOUT SIDEWALL INSULATION

Sidewall insulation can pose difficulties if you plan to blow it into the stud spaces in a frame residence. If a vapor barrier can be installed on the heated side without affecting the historic building materials, then proceed with the insulation project. If not, then consider not using sidewall insulation at all. Without a vapor barrier, the insulation will get wet as moisture from the inside air condenses in the wall where it meets the drier outside air in cold climates in the winter. As a result, the insulation is ineffective, paint will not adhere to the siding, and damage may occur to the walls.

If walls already have blown-in insulation and no vapor barriers, install vented (louvered or screened) plugs on the exterior of the house. A pair of two-inch diameter plugs at each stud space at each floor will provide some needed ventilation.

Avoid furring-in the walls of masonry buildings to install rigid, or batt, insulation with a vapor barrier. If you do this, you will be changing the size and proportions of the rooms, and you will need to find a sensitive way to address window and door trim. What you gain in energy savings is usually not worth the architectural or monetary cost.

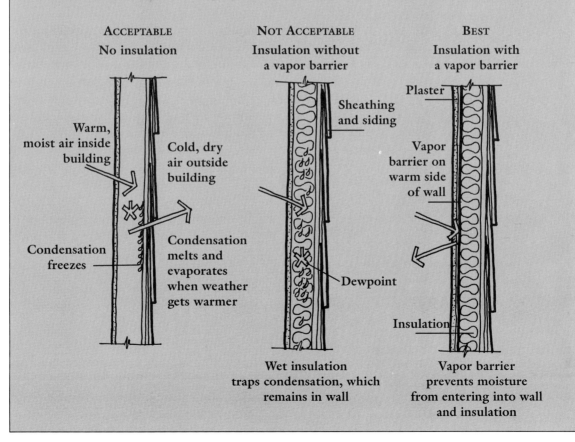

ACCEPTABLE
No insulation

Warm, moist air inside building

Cold, dry air outside building

Condensation freezes

Condensation melts and evaporates when weather gets warmer

NOT ACCEPTABLE
Insulation without a vapor barrier

Sheathing and siding

Dewpoint

Wet insulation traps condensation, which remains in wall

BEST
Insulation with a vapor barrier

Plaster

Vapor barrier on warm side of wall

Insulation

Vapor barrier prevents moisture from entering into wall and insulation filters several times during each season they are in use.

You can take a personal role in energy conservation by adapting yourself to a wide range of temperatures. Wear a sweater when it is cold or very lightweight clothing when the weather is hot, for instance, and adjust thermostats lower in the winter and higher in the summer. During cold months minimize the amount of moisture released in the house by cooking with lids on pots and limiting bath and shower times. This measure will help preserve the house, and you will quickly become accustomed to the lower humidity. If your furnace has a humidifier, turn it down or off.

After considering these simple activities, you will need to assess the house's insulation requirements. Is previously added insulation adequate? If none exists, add attic insulation first, followed by basement and crawl space insulation, along with duct and pipe insulation and a "blanket" for your hot water heater. Be aware that it is possible to over-insulate a historic house, rendering its structure and finishes unable to breathe. Always provide adequate ventilation for kitchens, bathrooms, laundry equipment and areas, attics, basements and crawl spaces. (See page 180 for more information on attic insulation and page 172 on basement insulation.)

Install and use dampers in fireplaces and avoid procedures that result in little, if any, energy savings, such as lowering ceilings. This not only renders little in terms of conservation, it can cause significant damage to the historic character of the house.

FURNISHINGS AND DECOR

Some general rules should govern decisions made regarding window treatments, carpets, rugs and other floor coverings, furniture styles and types, wallpapers and other wall coverings, and paint colors, techniques and schemes. These important features and treatments help define the character of historic houses.

First conduct a study of the period and style of the house to determine the type of furnishings and decor it might have had. Consider the likely lifestyle and income level of the early occupants and the historical availability of certain styles and types of furnishings in your area. The research you conducted earlier will assist you here, because much of this type of information can be ascertained from oral and written sources. This exercise can be interesting, fun and very rewarding.

After you have finished your research, one of your first concerns most likely will be what to do to the wood and plaster surfaces. In many cases, all that is needed is cleaning with a mild detergent, water and a sponge. If paint or wallpaper must be removed, become familiar with the best techniques for:

- Removing the coating properly and safely
- Preparing the surface for repainting or refinishing
- Applying new wallpaper, coats of paint or other finish

Always test your removal method in an inconspicuous spot. In repainting, you should use paint types specifically formulated for use on the material you are painting and follow the manufacturer's instructions (see page 156 for additional information on painting). Excellent sources of information on identifying, preserving, repairing and reproducing interior decorative techniques are available (see Further Reading).

When you are ready to plan your furnishings, consider using the general types of furnishings and decoration you believe the early occupants of the house would have had. These items do not have to be antiques but can be reproductions or contemporary furnishings compatible in design and color with the house. Avoid using materials and finishes that dominate the interior and are out of character with the house or its style. It would be an error, for example, to use richly detailed Victorian fabrics and furnishings in a Craftsman-style house, if what you are striving for is an authentic look.

This is not to say that furniture from an earlier or later period is never appropriate. Most of us have some family pieces or furniture of recent design that will work well nearly anywhere. In fact, some very successful house rehabilitation projects feature appropriately scaled modern furnishings and compatible contemporary finishes and colors as a counterpoint to a Victorian or other period interior. Finally, do not cover up significant architectural details with furniture or fabric.

Living room after rehabilitation. Historical and physical research revealed that windows in the neighborhood, typically two-over-two double-hung sash, were finished with simple panels of lace. The plaster was repaired, the woodwork repainted, the floor refinished and a new storm-screen door added in a color compatible to the trim color of the house.

FURTHER READING

Organized by chapter title, the following publications will prove useful to anyone needing further information about historic preservation, old houses, their style and their rehabilitation.

Why, What and How to Preserve

Fitch, James Marston. *American Building 1: The Historical Forces That Shaped It.* 2nd ed. New York: Schocken Books, 1966.

Greiff, Constance M. *Lost America: From the Atlantic to the Mississippi.* Princeton, N.J.: Pyne Press, 1971.

————. *Lost America: From the Mississippi to the Pacific.* Princeton, N.J.: Pyne Press, 1972.

Hosmer, Charles B., Jr. *Presence of the Past.* New York: G. P. Putnam's Sons, 1965.

————. *Preservation Comes of Age: From Williamsburg to the National Trust, 1926–1949.* 2 vols. Charlottesville: University Press of Virginia, 1981.

Maddex, Diane, ed. *All About Old Buildings.* Washington, D.C.: Preservation Press, 1985.

Murtagh, William J. *Keeping Time.* Pittstown, N.J.: Main Street Press, 1988.

Special Committee on Historic Preservation, U.S. Conference of Mayors. Albert Rains and Laurence G. Henderson, eds. *With Heritage So Rich.* 1966. Rev. reprint. Washington, D.C.: Preservation Press, 1983.

Stipe, Robert E., and Antoinette J. Lee, eds. *The American Mosaic: Preserving a Nation's Heritage.* Washington, D.C.: U.S. Committee, International Council on Monuments and Sites, 1987.

Wrenn, Tony P., and Elizabeth D. Mulloy. *America's Forgotten Architecture.* National Trust for Historic Preservation. New York: Pantheon, 1976.

Learning About Old Houses

In studying historic houses, general surveys and histories of architecture are the best sources followed by more specific references about the style or time period of the house you are researching.

Barzun, Jacques, and Henry F. Graff. *The Modern Researcher.* 3rd ed. New York: Harcourt Brace Jovanovich, 1977.

Blumenson, John J.-G. *Identifying American Architecture: A Pictorial Guide to Styles and Terms, 1600–1945.* 2nd ed. Nashville, Tenn.: American Association for State and Local History, 1981.

Gowans, Alan. *The Comfortable House: North American Suburban Architecture 1890–1930.* Cambridge, Mass.: MIT Press, 1986.

————. *Images of American Living: Four Centuries of Architecture and Furniture as Cultural Expression.* New York: Harper and Row, 1964.

Harris, Cyril M., ed. *Dictionary of Architecture and Con-*

struction. New York: McGraw-Hill, 1975.

Howe, Barbara J., Delores A. Fleming, Emory L. Kemp and Ruth Ann Overbeck. *Houses and Homes: Exploring Their History.* The Nearby History Series. Nashville, Tenn.: American Association for State and Local History, 1987.

McAlester, Virginia, and Lee McAlester. *A Field Guide to American Houses.* New York: Alfred A. Knopf, 1984.

Maddex, Diane, ed. *Master Builders: A Guide to Famous American Architects.* Washington, D.C.: Preservation Press, 1985.

Poppeliers, John C., Allen S. Chambers and Nancy B. Schwartz. *What Style Is It?* Washington, D.C.: Preservation Press, 1983.

Rifkind, Carole. *A Field Guide to American Architecture.* New York: NAL Penguin, 1980.

Roth, Leland M. *A Concise History of American Architecture.* New York: Harper and Row, 1979.

Saylor, Henry H. *Dictionary of Architecture.* New York: John Wiley and Sons, 1952.

Stevenson, Katherine Cole, and H. Ward Jandl. *Houses by Mail: A Guide to Houses from Sears, Roebuck and Company.* Washington, D.C.: Preservation Press, 1986.

Tishler, William H., ed. *American Landscape Architecture: Designers and Places.* Washington, D.C.: Preservation Press, 1986.

Whiffen, Marcus. *American Architecture Since 1780: A Guide to the Styles.* Cambridge, Mass.: MIT Press, 1969.

Safeguarding Properties

Burns, John A., ed., and staff of the Historic American Buildings Survey and the Historic American Engineering Record, National Park Service, U.S. Department of the Interior. *Recording Historic Structures.* Washington, D.C.: American Institute of Architects Press, 1989.

Coughlin, Thomas. *Easements and Other Legal Techniques to Protect Historic Houses in Private Ownership.* Washington, D.C.: Historic House Association of America, 1981.

Diehl, Janet, and Thomas S. Barrett. *The Conservation Easement Handbook: Managing Land Conservation and Historic Preservation Easement Programs.* San Francisco: Trust for Public Land, and Alexandria, Va.: Land Trust Exchange, 1988.

Duerksen, Christopher J., ed. *A Handbook on Historic Preservation Law.* Washington, D.C.: Conservation Foundation and National Center for Preservation Law, 1983.

Kitchen, Judith L. *Characteristics of Effective Local Historic Preservation Legislation.*
Columbus: Ohio Historic Preservation Office, Ohio Historical Society, 1989.

Meder-Montgomery, Marilyn. *Preservation Easements: A Legal Mechanism for Protecting Cultural Resources.* Denver: Colorado Historical Society, 1984.

"How to Apply the National Register Criteria for Evaluation." *National Register Bulletin 15.* Washington, D.C.: National Park Service, U.S. Department of the Interior, 1990.

"Guidelines for Completing National Register of Historic Places Forms." *National Register Bulletin 16.* Washington, D.C.: National Park Service, U.S. Department of the Interior, 1986.

National Trust for Historic Preservation. *Landmark Yellow Pages: Where to Find All the Names, Addresses, Facts and Figures You Need.* Washington, D.C.: Preservation Press, 1990.

Wilson, Rex, and Gloria Loyola, eds. *Rescue Archeology.* Washington, D.C.: Preservation Press, 1982.

Financial Considerations

Architectural Conservation Trust for Massachusetts and Architectural Heritage Foundation. *The Revolving Fund Handbook.* Boston: Architectural Conservation Trust, 1979.

National Trust for Historic Preservation. *Economic Benefits of Preserving Old Buildings.* Washington, D.C.: Preservation Press, 1976.

Nielson, Sally E. *Investing in Old Buildings.* Portland, Maine: Greater Portland Landmarks, 1980.

Oldham, Sally G., Jayne F. Boyle and Stuart M. Ginsberg. *A Guide to Tax Advantaged Rehabilitation.* Washington, D.C.: National Trust for Historic Preservation, 1986.

Preserving America's Heritage: The Rehabilitation Investment Tax Credit. Cleveland, Ohio: Touche Ross and Co. and Ohio Historic Preservation Office, 1987.

Urban Land Institute. *Adaptive Use: Development Economics, Process and Profiles.* Washington, D.C.: author, 1978.

Ziegler, Arthur P., Jr., Leopold Adler II and Walter C. Kidney. *Revolving Funds for Historic Preservation: A Manual of Practice.* Pittsburgh: Ober Park Associate, 1975.

Before You Begin

Among these references are examples of successful local preservation guides designed for use by homeowners and well-prepared historic structure reports for houses.

Anderson Notter Associates and Historic Salem. *The Salem Handbook: A Renovation Guide for Homeowners.* Salem, Mass.: Historic Salem, 1977.

Chambers, J. Henry, AIA. *Cyclical Maintenance for Historic Buildings.* Washington, D.C.: National Park Service, U.S. Department of the Interior, 1976.

German Village Commission and German Village Society, with Benjamin D. Rickey and Co. and Schmeltz+Warren Design. *German Village Guidelines: Preserving Historic Architecture.* Columbus, Ohio: German Village Society, 1989.

Hume, Gary L., and W. Brown Morton III. *The Secretary of the Interior's Standards for Historic Preservation Projects, With Guidelines for Applying the Standards.* Revised. Washington, D.C.: U.S. Department of the Interior, 1990.

Kitchen, Judith L. *Old-Building Owner's Manual.* Columbus: Ohio Historic Preservation Office, Ohio Historical Society, 1983.

Mendel, Mesick, Cohen, Architects. *Fort Johnson, Amsterdam, New York: A Historic Structure Report, 1974–1975.* Washington, D.C.: U.S. Department of the Interior, 1978.

Phillips, Morgan W. *The Morse-Libby Mansion, Portland, Maine: A Report on Restoration Work, 1973–1977.* Washington, D.C.: National Park Service, U.S. Department of the Interior, 1977.

Pitts, Carolyn, Michael Fish, Hugh J. McCauley, AIA, and Trina Vaux. *The Cape May Handbook.* Philadelphia: Athenaeum of Philadelphia, 1977.

Reader's Digest Complete Do-It-Yourself Manual. Pleasantville, N.Y.: The Reader's Digest Association, 1977.

Rehab Right: How to Rehabilitate Your Oakland House Without Sacrificing Architectural Assets. Oakland, Calif.: City of Oakland Planning Department, 1978.

Simonson, Kaye Ellen, ed. *Maintaining Historic Buildings: An Annotated Bibliography.* Washington, D.C.: National Park Service, U.S. Department of the Interior, 1990.

Outside the Old House

A number of these books are useful for interior work as well.

Favretti, Rudy J., and Joy Putman Favretti. *Landscapes and Gardens for Historic Buildings: A Handbook for Reproducing and Creating Authentic Landscape Settings.* Nashville, Tenn.: American Association for State and Local History, 1978.

Fisher, Charles E., ed. *The Window Workbook for Historic Buildings.* Washington, D.C.: Historic Preservation Education Foundation, 1986.

Gayle, Margot, David W. Look, AIA, and John G. Waite. *Metals in America's*

Historic Buildings. Washington, D.C.: U.S. Department of the Interior, 1980.

Gratwick, R. T. *Dampness in Buildings.* 2nd ed. London: Crosby Lockwood Staples, 1974.

Grimmer, Anne E. *Keeping It Clean—Removing Exterior Dirt, Paint, Stains and Graffiti from Historic Masonry Buildings.* Washington, D.C.: National Park Service, U.S. Department of the Interior, 1988.

Johnson, Ed. *Old House Woodwork Restoration.* Englewood Cliffs, N.J.: Prentice-Hall, 1983.

Litchfield, Michael. *Renovation.* New York: John Wiley and Sons, 1982.

London, Mark. *Masonry: How to Care for Old and Historic Brick and Stone.* Washington, D.C.: Preservation Press, 1988.

McHargue, Georgess, and Michael Roberts. *A Field Guide to Conservation Archaeology in North America.* Philadelphia: Lippincott, 1977.

Melville, Ian A., and Ian A. Gordon. *The Repair and Maintenance of Houses.* London: Estates Gazette Limited, 1973.

Miller, Kevin H., ed. *Paint Color Research and Restoration of Historic Paint.* Ottawa, Canada: Association for Preservation Technology, 1977.

Moss, Roger W., and Gail Caskey Winkler. *Victorian Exterior Decoration: How to Paint Your Nineteenth-Century American House Historically.* New York: Henry Holt, 1987.

National Park Service. *Respectful Rehabilitation: Answers to Your Questions About Old Buildings.* Washington, D.C.: Preservation Press, 1982.

National Trust for Historic Preservation. *Old and New Architecture: Design Relationship.* Washington, D.C.: Preservation Press, 1980.

Noel Hume, Ivor. *Historical Archaeology.* New York: Alfred A. Knopf, 1969.

Stephen, George. *New Life for Old Houses.* Rev. ed. Washington, D.C.: Preservation Press, 1989.

Inside the Old House

Fisher, Charles E., Michael Auer and Anne Grimmer, eds. *The Interiors Handbook for Historic Buildings.* Washington, D.C.: Historic Preservation Education Foundation, 1988.

Frangiamore, Catherine Lynn. *Wallpapers in Historic Preservation.* Washington, D.C.: National Park Service, U.S. Department of the Interior, 1977.

Grimmer, Anne, ed. *Historic Building Interiors: An Annotated Bibliography.* Washington, D.C.: National Park Service, U.S. Department of the Interior, 1989.

Moss, Roger W. *Lighting for Historic Buildings.* Washington, D.C.: Preservation Press, 1988.

Nylander, Jane C. *Fabrics for Historic Buildings.* 4th ed. Washington, D.C.: Preservation Press, 1990.

Nylander, Richard C. *Wallpapers for Historic Buildings.* Washington, D.C.: Preservation Press, 1983.

Shivers, Natalie. *Walls and Molding: How to Care for Old and Historic Wood and Plaster.* Washington, D.C.: Preservation Press, 1990.

Von Rosenstiel, Helene, and Gail Caskey Winkler. *Floor Coverings for Historic Buildings.* Washington, D.C.: Preservation Press, 1988.

Seale, William. *Recreating the Historic House Interior.* Nashville, Tenn.: American Association for State and Local History, 1979.

———. *The Tasteful Interlude: American Interiors Through the Camera's Eye, 1860–1917.* New York: Praeger, 1975.

Winkler, Gail Caskey. Introduction to *The Well-Appointed Bath: Authentic Plans and Fixtures from the Early 1900s.* Reprint of two early catalogs. Washington, D.C.: Preservation Press, 1989.

Winkler, Gail Caskey, and Roger W. Moss. *Victorian Interior Decoration: American Interiors 1830–1900.* New York: Henry Holt, 1986.

Periodicals

Association for Preservation Technology Bulletin. Published quarterly. Fredericksburg, Va.: Association for Preservation Technology International, 1969–present.

Historic Preservation. Published bimonthly. Washington, D.C.: National Trust for Historic Preservation.

Historic Preservation News. Published monthly. Washington, D.C.: National Trust for Historic Preservation.

Old-House Journal. Published monthly. Brooklyn, N.Y.: Old-House Journal Corporation, 1973–present.

Traditional Building: Historical Products for Today's Professional. Published bimonthly. Brooklyn, N.Y.: Clem Labine, 1988–present.

National Park Service. *Preservation Briefs.* Washington, D.C.: U.S. Department of the Interior, 1975–present.

No. 1 The Cleaning and Waterproof Coating of Masonry Buildings

No. 2 Repointing Mortar Joints in Historic Brick Buildings

No. 3 Conserving Energy in Historic Buildings

No. 4 Roofing for Historic Buildings

No. 5 Preservation of Historic Adobe Buildings

No. 6 Dangers of Abrasive Cleaning to Historic Buildings

No. 8 Aluminum and Vinyl Siding on Historic Buildings

No. 9 The Repair of Historic Wooden Windows

No. 10 Exterior Paint Problems on Historic Woodwork

No. 13 The Repair and Thermal Upgrading of Historic Steel Windows

No. 14 New Exterior Additions to Historic Buildings: Preservation Concerns

No. 15 Preservation of Historic Concrete: Problems and General Approaches

No. 16 The Use of Substitute Materials on Historic Building Exteriors

No. 17 Architectural Character: Identifying the Visual Aspects of Historic Buildings as an Aid to Preserving Their Character

No. 18 Rehabilitating Interiors in Historic Buildings: Identifying and Preserving Character-defining Elements

No. 19 The Repair and Replacement of Historic Wooden Shingle Roofs

No. 20 The Preservation of Historic Barns

No. 21 Repairing Historic Flat Plaster — Walls and Ceilings

No. 22 The Preservation and Repair of Historic Stucco

No. 23 Preserving Historic Ornamental Plaster

WHERE TO GO FOR HELP

Whatever part of the country your house is in, you will find that some of the best advice comes from contacts you make in your quest for knowledge and just plain information. These contacts may be through public or private services but they will all be people who are anxious to help.

LOCAL

Your village, town, city, borough, township, county or parish historic preservation office or agency, if it is not an independent division, will most likely be housed in a planning or community development office. Check here first for information about programs for which you may qualify. If there is no historic preservation coordinator in your local government, then check with local building code officials for information on rehabilitation work. You may also want to check with your state historic preservation office.

Similarly, locate your local historic preservation organization or local historical society in seeking assistance. If you live in a historic neighborhood or historic district that has a neighborhood organization, by all means contact this group with your immediate concerns. If you have difficulty locating any organizations, check with your local library.

Students from Hampton Institute in Virginia building a stairway in 1899. (Library of Congress)

STATE

Every state, most territories and the District of Columbia have an official state historic preservation office usually housed within a state agency. This is the place to find educational information: what has been nominated to and listed in the National Register of Historic Places or the statewide inventory of properties significant in history, architecture and archeology; projects qualifying for federal tax benefits; information on funding sources; federal involvement in projects that will affect National Register–eligible properties; advice on restoration and rehabilitation; and information on locating historic preservation organizations in your area of the state.

A list of all state historic preservation offices is available by writing to:

National Conference of State Historic
    Preservation Officers
444 North Capitol Street, N.W.
Suite 332
Washington, D.C. 20001

In addition to the state historic preservation office, most states have private statewide historic preservation organizations. These range from small, all-volunteer groups to large, professionally staffed associations. Ask your state historic preservation office for information about a statewide organization.

NATIONAL

The National Park Service, which is part of the U.S. Department of the Interior, is the federal government's historic preservation agency. It is responsible for the National Register of Historic Places, the tax benefits program, dissemination of technical information and a wide range of historic preservation–related services to other federal agencies, to the state historic preservation offices and to the public. The general address and regional office addresses are:

National Park Service
U.S. Department of the
    Interior
P.O. Box 37127
Washington, D.C. 20013-7127

Mid-Atlantic Regional Office
Office of Cultural Programs
200 Chestnut Street
Second Floor
Philadelphia, Pa. 19106

Southeast Regional Office
Preservation Services
    Division
75 Spring Street, S.W.
Room 1140
Atlanta, Ga. 30303

Rocky Mountain Regional
    Office
Division of Cultural
    Resources
655 Parfet Street
P.O. Box 25287
Denver, Colo. 80225

Western Regional Office
National Historic
    Preservation Programs
450 Golden Gate Avenue
P.O. Box 36063
San Francisco, Calif. 94102

Alaska Regional Office
Cultural Resources
    Division
2525 Gambell Street
Room 107
Anchorage, Alaska 99505

The Advisory Council on Historic Preservation reviews and comments on federally assisted and federally licensed undertakings that will have an effect on properties either listed in the National Register of Historic Places or eligible for listing. Its headquarters address is:

Advisory Council on Historic Preservation
1100 Pennsylvania Avenue, N.W.
Suite 809
Washington, D.C. 20004

The Department of Housing and Urban Development offers a number of housing assistance programs, many based on need. While none is tailored specifically to preservation, most programs would include funding for repairs and maintenance, both of which constitute what would be considered preservation. In addition, local authorities receive monies through the Community Development Block Grant program. For further information contact your local housing authority or write to:

U.S. Department of Housing and Urban Development
Historic Preservation Officer
Environmental Management Division
451 7th Street, S.W.
Washington, D.C. 20410

The National Trust for Historic Preservation, a membership organization, chartered by the U.S. Congress to encourage historic preservation activities throughout the country, has numerous programs, including its own house museums; a book-publishing arm, The Preservation Press; a magazine, newspaper and journal; financial assistance programs; conferences and training sessions; and the Center for Historic Houses. It operates seven regional and field offices. Contact:

Center for Historic Houses
National Trust for Historic
    Preservation
1785 Massachusetts Avenue,
    N.W.
Washington, D.C. 20036

Northeast Regional Office
45 School Street
4th Floor
Boston, Mass. 02108

Mid-Atlantic Regional Office
6401 Germantown Avenue
Philadelphia, Pa. 19144

Southern Regional Office
456 King Street
Charleston, S.C. 29403

Midwest Regional Office
53 West Jackson Boulevard
Suite 1135
Chicago, Ill. 60604

Mountains/Plains
    Regional Office
511 16th Street
Suite 700
Denver, Colo. 80202

Texas/New Mexico
    Field Office
511 Main Street
Suite 606
Fort Worth, Tex. 76102

Western Regional Office
One Sutter Street
Suite 900
San Francisco, Calif. 94104

In addition to the National Trust, there are numerous private national organizations that focus on some aspect of historic preservation. Among these are the following:

American Association for
    State and Local History
172 Second Avenue, North
Nashville, Tenn. 37201

American Institute of
    Architects
Committee on Historic
    Resources
1735 New York Avenue, N.W.
Washington, D.C. 20006

American Society
    of Interior Designers
Historic Preservation
    Committee
608 Massachusetts Avenue, N.E.
Washington, D.C. 20002

American Society
    of Landscape Architects
Committee on Historic
    Preservation
4401 Connecticut Avenue, N.W.
5th Floor
Washington, D.C. 20008-2302

Association for Preservation
   Technology International
Box 8178
Fredericksburg, Va. 22404

Garden Clubs of America
Conservation Committee
598 Madison Avenue
New York, N.Y. 10022

National Center
   for Preservation Law
1333 Connecticut Avenue, N.W.
Suite 300
Washington, D.C. 20036

Society for American
   Archaeology
808 17th Street, N.W.
Suite 200
Washington, D.C. 20006

Society of Architectural
   Historians
1232 Pine Street
Philadelphia, Pa. 19107-5944

The Victorian Society in
   America
219 South Sixth Street
Philadelphia, Pa. 19106

For advice about raising funds through private philan-
thropies, two excellent sources are the following, both of
which publish directories:

The Foundation Center
79 Fifth Avenue
New York, N.Y. 10003

The Taft Group
12300 Twinbrook Parkway
Suite 450
Rockville, Md. 20852

Member of a summer team of
Historic American Buildings
Survey delineators at
Cliveden, Philadelphia, in
1972. (Jack Boucher, HABS)

GLOSSARY

Adobe Sun-dried brick.

Arcade Series of arches with their supports.

Arch Means of spanning an opening by using individual units of masonry to transfer the load outward and downward.

Architrave Lowest member of the classical entablature; also door or window trim.

Ashlar Squared stone blocks used in building.

Balloon Framing Wood framing with studs that are continuous from the first floor to the roof.

Balustrade Railing at a stairway, porch or roof that is supported by individual decorative posts called balusters.

Bargeboard Decorative boards located at the inverted-V end of a gable.

Bay Window Building projection supported by a foundation and containing windows.

Beam Major horizontal structural member in frame construction.

Belt Course Horizontal band, often of contrasting masonry, around a building.

Board-and-Batten Siding of vertical or horizontal boards with narrow vertical strips, or battens, at the intersections covering the joint.

Box Gutter Gutter contained within a projection of the house's cornice.

Braced Framing Wood framing having diagonal braces; a common type of mortise-and-tenon framing.

Bracket Supporting element projecting from a wall under a cornice or other feature.

Cantilever Projecting overhang, upper floor or beam.

Capital Uppermost part of a classical column or other support.

Casement Window Window with sash pivoting outward on a vertical hinge at the jamb.

Caulking Flexible material used to weatherproof or otherwise protect the juncture between two surfaces.

Colonnade Series of columns supporting an entablature.

Column Vertical round support, generally having a base, shaft and capital.

Coping Capping covering the top of a wall or parapet.

Cornice Uppermost member of a classical entablature; projecting section at the juncture of wall and roof or ceiling.

Cresting Decoration, usually metal, along the top of a roof.

Dentil One of a row of small rectangular blocks forming a molding below a cornice.

Dormer Structure, usually with windows, that projects from a roof.

Double-Hung Window Window having sash that operate vertically past each other; described by the number of lights in the upper and lower sash, for instance, six-over-six (6/6), nine-over-six (9/6), two-over-two (2/2).

Eaves Section of roof that projects over an exterior wall.

Entablature Part of a structure above the classical column, including the architrave, frieze and cornice.

Eyebrow Window Roof dormer having no sides and formed by raising a small section of the roof.

Facade Front or "face" of a building.

Fanlight Fixed window sash above a door, often curved.

Finial Decorative vertical roof ornament.

Flashing Waterproof material, often metal, which makes an intersection of materials weathertight; found at all roof openings.

Foundation Structure upon which a building rests.

Frieze Middle section of a classical entablature, sometimes decorated or with windows.

Gable Roof Single-pitched roof with end walls that are pointed at the top.

Gambrel Roof Double-pitched roof with end walls that are pointed at the top.

Half Story Habitable space above a house's cornice; usually formed by dormers.

Half-Timbering Type of early frame construction in which the spaces between the heavy timbers are filled with brick, stone or plaster, sometimes called "nogging"; also used to describe a decorative treatment of this type.

Hipped Roof Roof having a slope on all four sides.

Hoodmold Decorative projecting trim above a window.

Jamb Side of a window or door opening.

Joist One of a series of smaller horizontal members supporting a floor.

Lath Strips or sheets of wood or metal attached to the structural members to serve as a backing for plaster.

Light Individual pane of glass in a window or door.

Lintel Beam supported on posts or sections of a wall to span a window or door opening.

Mansard Roof Double-pitched roof in which the lower pitch is nearly vertical and the upper nearly horizontal.

Molding Usually decorative strip of wood or other material.

Mortise-and-Tenon Early wood joinery in which a "tongue" (tenon) fits into a recess (mortise); a peg secures the joint.

Mullion Vertical division between a series of windows.

Muntin Vertical or horizontal divisions between lights in a window or door sash.

Order Form of the column and its capital in classical architecture; the Greek orders are Doric, Ionic and Corinthian.

Oriel Projection on a house, usually on an upper floor, containing windows and supported by brackets or other means.

Palladian Window Window with an arched center section flanked by lower flat-topped sections.

Parapet Wall that rises above the edge of a roof.

Party Wall Common wall shared by two dwelling units in a double house or row house.

Pediment In classical architecture, the triangular upper part of a gable roof.

Pilaster Squared vertical wall projection, often with a capital.

Plasterboard Manufactured sheets of plaster between cardboard; also called drywall, sheetrock or wallboard.

Platform Framing Wood framing having single-story studs that rest on the floors.

Portico Porch supported by columns; usually with a pediment.

Post Major vertical supporting element in frame construction.

Rafter One of a series of smaller structural members forming a roof and to which a roof covering is applied.

Rubble Undressed, broken stone used in construction.

Sash Parts of a window or door that hold the glass, or lights, and generally operate to open and close.

Scrollwork Ornamental woodwork produced by a jigsaw; also referred to as gingerbread or spindlework.

Sheathing Boards applied to the exterior of a structural frame to receive the roofing material and siding.

Siding Exterior wall covering applied to sheathing.

Sill Beam or member located at the top of a foundation and upon which the house rests; also bottom member of a window or door opening.

Soffit Underside of an eaves, lintel, arch or other element.

Spalling Deterioration and falling away of masonry due to moisture penetration or other cause.

Stucco Exterior finish, often textured, composed of lime and sand with some portland cement.

Stud Wall Wall formed by smaller vertical structural members in a series.

Tie Rod Metal rod in tension, used to tie or brace a structure; seen on the exterior as a bearing plate, sometimes in an ornamental shape.

Transom Operable solid panel or sash over a door to provide ventilation.

Vapor Barrier Continuous sheet of impermeable material that prevents interior moisture from reaching insulation.

Veranda Long, often two-story, porch that runs along the front or side of a building.

Wainscot Decorative treatment, in wood paneling or other material, given to the lower part of an interior wall; also called a dado.

Water Table Projection, usually of masonry, above a foundation to direct water away from it.

Weatherstripping Material used to help block air infiltration around doors and windows.

Window Frame Fixed interior and exterior parts of a window designed to hold the sash.

INDEX

203

AUTHOR

J udith Kitchen heads the Technical and Review Services Department of the Ohio Historic Preservation Office under the Ohio Historical Society and initiated that office's very popular Building Doctor program in 1979. Also an adjunct associate professor of architecture at Ohio State University, Kitchen received her professional training in architecture at Ohio State, in architectural history at the University of Virginia and, more recently, in real estate and finance at Ohio State. She has written several books, including *Architecture: Columbus, Characteristics of Effective Local Historic Preservation Legislation* and the *Old-Building Owner's Manual,* for which she received a Certificate of Commendation from the National Trust for Historic Preservation in 1985. She has rehabilitated an old house and is active in several local historic preservation organizations.

Fence at Coburn Tyler House, Camden, Maine, an important exterior feature of this site. (Cervin Robinson, HABS)